**Applied Research for
Sustainable Change**

Applied Research for Sustainable Change

A Guide for
Education Leaders

Sharon M. Ravitch
Nicole Mittenfelner Carl

HARVARD EDUCATION PRESS
Cambridge, Massachusetts

Copyright © 2019 by the President and Fellows of Harvard College

All rights reserved. No part of this publication may be reproduced or transmitted in any form or by any means, electronic or mechanical, including photocopy, recording, or any information storage and retrieval systems, without permission in writing from the publisher.

Paperback ISBN 978-1-68253-394-9
Library Edition ISBN 978-1-68253-395-6

Library of Congress Cataloging-in-Publication Data

Names: Ravitch, Sharon M., author. | Carl, Nicole Mittenfelner, author.
Title: Applied research for sustainable change : a guide for education leaders / Sharon M. Ravitch, Nicole Mittenfelner Carl.
Description: Cambridge, Massachusetts : Harvard Education Press, [2019] | Includes index.
Identifiers: LCCN 2019017564| ISBN 9781682533949 (pbk.) | ISBN 9781682533956 (library binding)
Subjects: LCSH: Action research in education. | School management and organization. | Educational leadership. | Research--Methodology. | Qualitative research.
Classification: LCC LB1028.24 .R38 2019 | DDC 370.72--dc23 LC record available at https://lccn.loc.gov/2019017564

Published by Harvard Education Press,
an imprint of the Harvard Education Publishing Group

Harvard Education Press
8 Story Street
Cambridge, MA 02138

Cover Design: Endpaper Studio
Cover Photo: asiseeit/Getty Images

The typefaces used in this book are Candide, Avenir, and Gotham.

For Susan Lytle,
inspiration, kindred spirit, comrade, sister
—SMR

For my mother,
a master teacher
—NMC

CONTENTS

INTRODUCTION
Breaking the Tyranny of Numbers — 1

1. Leading Through Learning and Collaboration — 9
2. Organizational Culture and Norms in Applied Research — 29
3. Designing Applied Research — 49
4. Creating Collaborative Research Teams — 81
5. Collecting Useful and Actionable Data — 103
6. Conducting Data Analysis — 135
7. Disseminating Findings, Sustaining Action, and Professional Development — 161

CONCLUSION
Applied Research and Sustainable Organizational Change — 179

APPENDIX
List of Practices to Get Started — 183

RESOURCES — 185

A	Additional Readings on Brave Spaces	185
B	Topics for Focus Walks	187
C	Flash Focus Group Topics and Questions	188
D	Applied Research Design Template	191
E	Questions to Guide Personal and Group Discussion of Biases and Blind Spots	193
F	Example of an Interview Instrument for Teachers, Counselors, and Advisers, First Draft	194
G	Potential Aspects to Consider During School-Based Observations	196
H	Template for Open-Ended Fieldnotes Instrument	197
I	Example of a Student Focus Group Instrument	198
J	Example of a Survey Sent to Teachers	200
K	Sample Data Collection Plan and Timeline	201
L	Template for Aligning Methods to Research Questions	202
M	Software Programs and Other Resources for Recording and Organizing Data	203
N	Examples of Data Summary Forms	204
O	Example of a Code List and Definitions	206
P	Example of a Data Analysis Plan	207

Glossary	209
Notes	215
Acknowledgments	221
About the Authors	225
Index	229

INTRODUCTION

Breaking the Tyranny of Numbers

IN A NATION where education and social policy are so intertwined, the role of educational leaders has become increasingly complex and externally driven. To meet these challenges as an educational leader, you need a mindset and a capacity for designing and implementing valid research. Education experts debate what constitutes effective, evidence-based practice for educational leaders and the kinds of research that these educators should conduct in schools, districts, and other organizations. We wrote *Applied Research for Sustainable Change: A Guide for Education Leaders* in response to these debates and challenges.

This book makes the case for applied **qualitative research** in schools, districts, and other educational organizations. Applied research integrates theoretical research and actual practice, enabling educators to assess their practices and improve them in light of context-specific data. In applied research, questions emerge from practice, and practitioners design research studies to collect and analyze data (often in relation to existing quantitative data) that respond to these questions within their organizational or institutional contexts. A primary goal of applied research is to generate useful knowledge to inform decision-making and change efforts. Throughout the book, we describe applied research that educational leaders can conduct with their colleagues to better understand

and to improve their own practice as leaders and their schools, districts, and systems. This kind of research must be efficient to be sustainable. For this reason, we ground our discussion in concrete examples and, at the end of each chapter, suggest practices that you can use to get started.

Our suggested approach to educational leadership is supported by, and contributes to, applied research. This approach, like qualitative research more broadly, emphasizes critical listening, authentic engagement, a broad and receptive perspective, humility, empathy, ethics, collaboration, and curiosity. Using applied research to drive local (site-based) educational change means understanding and valuing local knowledge, experiences, and priorities. Through this research, educational leaders can use contextualized, site-generated data to help shift the current neoliberal, top-down approach to schooling that is foisted on US educators (even those working in independent and private schools). Throughout the book, we explore the primary role of collaboration in educational innovation.

This book focuses on how you and other educational professionals can champion and conduct applied research. There is scant literature on how leadership-level practitioners (particularly school and district leaders) and their colleagues conduct site-based research and how this research influences these educators' leadership practices.[1]

This book is the outgrowth of twenty-plus years of our own work teaching, conducting, and facilitating practitioner-led research in public schools, districts, and independent schools and our close work with other educators as they studied their own educational situations and contexts. We worked together for many years at a school-based applied research center with a mission to use this research to cultivate local educational change. The examples in the book are based on our experiences working with a variety of educational leaders in multiple educational settings, and the resources provided at the end of this book (and online) have been developed from these experiences.

Leaders can use applied research to push against the norms and power dynamics that create staleness and powerlessness in their schools and to increase respect, trust, and buy-in from colleagues and other stakeholders.

Applied research can generate data that address how schools—and the people who work within them—are being pressured and constrained by the tyranny of numbers. We view this constraint as a tyranny because the current education system in many ways forces professionals to ostensibly paint by numbers (gathered by others) rather than giving them the freedom to build knowledge creatively. We seek to interrupt the current deprofessionalization that pervades much of the educational system in the United States and to promote a hopeful, critical, and substantive approach to more effective schooling practices. This book presents a way to shift the ethos in most schools. Today, leaders typically feel forced to accept metrics that are unconnected to their own circumstances and that are employed in sloppy, sometimes deleterious ways. We instead focus on how applied qualitative research can help you and other educational leaders build a more holistic understanding of schools and the range of stakeholder priorities and experiences within them.

As the term implies, applied research seeks to have a direct application. The approach can combine quantitative, qualitative, and **mixed methods research**. In this book, *applied research* refers primarily to qualitative approaches in combination with preexisting quantitative data because schools and other educational institutions are already awash with numerical data and metrics. You may have heard of other applied research approaches, including action research, practitioner research, and practitioner action research. The approach we put forth in this book is similar to those approaches, but also varies. Our approach to sustainable change involves a collaborative team that is a part of all the applied research processes and outcomes. Another key aspect of our approach is professional development. We present ways for applied research to be integrated into professional development opportunities; the research findings inform and are informed by professional development practices. This is why we refer to our approach as applied research.

Applied research fosters sustainable change, that is, lasting change that benefits all stakeholders, in at least three ways. First, it helps people develop a more contextualized and holistic understanding of an issue. Second, it seeks out multiple perspectives from educational stakeholders. Finally, it offers a continuous cycle of improvement, so that the actions that result from the research and the original presenting issues are monitored to make sure they are addressing the desired goals.

THE STRUCTURE OF THE BOOK

In this book, we aim to help you and other educators use applied research to gather issue-specific information to make sustainable changes in your own areas of concern. To make this process accessible, we describe in every chapter one or two real-world examples of educational leaders engaging in applied research. Although these examples come from our work with school leaders, we use pseudonyms and fictitious names of schools and districts to protect the individuals' identities. The leaders have various positions and include superintendents, assistant superintendents, principals, assistant principals, district coaches, directors of instruction, heads of independent schools, teachers, and school counselors. We looked at leaders in a variety of settings throughout the United States, including suburban and urban districts, charter schools, underserved public districts, and elite independent schools. The issues that these educational leaders address through applied research vary widely, for example, a districtwide focus on school discipline, faculty resistance to pedagogical change, and a persistent plateau in standardized test scores. Other applied research topics include the creation of a dual-credit program, low parent attendance at conferences, preparation for a school accreditation, ways to incorporate conceptual teaching practices, and an assessment of a district's professional development offerings and how dialogue is facilitated.

At the beginning of each chapter, we present questions for you to consider, and we address these throughout the chapter. We try to show you, in a straightforward way, what applied research is and what it looks like in practice. To that end, we present many illustrations of the processes we describe in each chapter and include concrete tips for putting these into practice. Furthermore, at the end of each chapter, we detail ways for you to get started applying what we have just discussed. The appendix includes all these practices for your reference.

Key terms are in bold at their first mention and are defined in the text. For your convenience, we include a glossary of these boldfaced terms at the end of the book. Finally, we include a resources section at the end of the book, where you will find reproducible templates, examples, further readings, and more information about specific topics. These resources are action oriented, specific, and easily customizable.

OVERVIEW OF CHAPTERS

Chapter 1 defines the concepts of applied research for sustainable change and leadership through collaboration. We overview the major applied research processes and, to show how this research is developed, describe how a superintendent involved principals in an applied research project and in individual projects at their schools. We discuss four mindsets that are vital for educational leaders to cultivate if they want to engage in applied research for sustainable change. Leaders need to situate themselves as learners, reconsider data and research, view collaboration as integral to professional excellence and development, and recognize and challenge the status quo. The chapter concludes with practices you can use to cultivate these mindsets with your colleagues and staff.

Chapter 2 helps educational leaders consider the important roles of culture and norms in their organization in a way that can help leaders both anticipate barriers to change and design applied research projects that are more relevant, collaborative, and sustainable. The chapter presents multiple practices that you, as an educational leader, can use to examine aspects of your organization.

Chapter 3 describes important considerations for applied research design. For example, leaders need to decide on the research topic and goals, develop guiding research questions, understand the existing knowledge about an issue, choose appropriate research methods, select the participants in a study, and plan for the **validity** of the research. They also have to allocate the time and resources for the research. In this chapter, we also detail ethical considerations that leaders and research teams need to actively plan for, and we describe ways to align applied research with existing data sources. Examples provided in this chapter make these various considerations more concrete. The chapter concludes with three practices to guide leaders through the design of sustainable applied research.

Chapter 4 discusses collaborative research teams. We describe three key processes for collaborative research, including a multiple-perspective approach, a commitment to shared learning and knowledge exchange, and an openness to change. This chapter discusses important considerations for forming an effective **applied research team** and examines how collaboratively defining and revisiting the goals, roles, and norms of a team is central to leading such a team. We also present an example of how a director of curriculum and instruction facilitates and successfully leads an applied research ream with competing priorities. The chapter concludes by detailing several practices for building trust and fostering **reflexivity** among team members.

In chapter 5, we examine how a study's research questions determine the methods of data collection needed. We describe the primary data collection methods used in applied research, such as focus groups, **photovoice**, and mapping. The chapter also discusses the **research instruments** for gathering data. Revisiting the example of an assistant principal and his applied research team who were studying plateaued test scores, the chapter describes how the team collected data to answer their research questions. Chapter 5 also discusses methods for promoting research validity during data collection. For example, you can check in periodically with the participants in your study, incorporate multiple perspectives and data sources, use reflexive strategies, and collaborate with your team members. We also show how a superintendent uses these validity processes during her applied research study. The chapter concludes with specific practices to help your team begin to collect useful and valid data.

Chapter 6 defines data analysis and discusses three main processes of data analysis for applied research. The chapter also describes how teams can collaboratively develop thematic findings. Throughout the chapter, you will find tips to make these processes easier and will see examples of analysis in action. We will also show you how one research team analyzed its data and developed findings. We'll outline some practical steps you and your team can take in analyzing your data. The chapter concludes with specific practices to help you and your team get started analyzing data.

Chapter 7 focuses on the central question of what to do with your research. To answer this question, we revisit the goals of applied research (and this book): local, sustainable change. We then detail ways to disseminate your research, present your data and findings, and implement action. We describe how one research team accomplished these goals. This chapter also describes different ways to structure reports and presentations, invite feedback, and address dissent.

We conclude this book by reflecting on the importance of applied research to generate sustainable educational change. The conclusion also discusses how the applied research processes themselves provide numerous professional development opportunities in addition to the opportunities stemming from the focus of the research.

ONE

Leading Through Learning and Collaboration

CONDUCTING APPLIED RESEARCH helps leaders make relevant and informed decisions that lead to more holistic and effective approaches to student learning, psychosocial development, **capacity building**, and professional development in schools and districts so that educational organizations better meet the needs of students, teachers, and staff. In this chapter, we define applied research for sustainable change and show how such research also contributes to a leader's credibility, efficacy, and professionalism. Furthermore, this chapter presents an approach to transformative, relational leadership in which collaboration with colleagues, staff members, and other educational stakeholders is a key component.

We begin this chapter by introducing our approach to educational change. The approach involves leading through learning and collaboration with colleagues and other educational stakeholders. The chapter then presents a bird's-eye view of the applied research cycle to overview the processes involved in this approach. To help bring these processes to light, we share a brief example of an applied research project conducted by a superintendent and the principals in a district that sought sustainable organizational change. We then articulate the central leadership mindsets that guide applied research processes, specifically the importance situating oneself as a learner, reconsidering preexisting data and research, viewing collaboration as integral to professional development, and challenging the status quo. The chapter also discusses why applied research in education is especially relevant in the current educational atmosphere of test-driven pedagogy and mass privatization and marketization. We conclude the chapter with suggestions for leaders who wish to cultivate the leadership mindsets central to applied research for sustainable change.

Throughout this chapter, we address the following questions:

- What does leading through learning and collaboration entail?
- Why is applied research useful in educational settings?
- What are qualitative data, and how can they be used in educational institutions?
- What is a **community of practice**?
- How can educational leaders foster communities of practice?
- What are some key mindsets for effective leadership?
- How do you start an applied research project?

THE BENEFITS OF A COLLABORATIVE LEARNER STANCE

A central premise and goal of this book is to help you, as an educational leader, position yourself and your colleagues as learners. Research shows that leaders are more successful when they adopt and model a learning stance. This means that you position yourself as an active learner who is curious about the perspectives and experiences of others, rather than as an all-knowing expert who simply disseminates information.[1] This stance challenges the expert-versus-learner tension so common in school and district hierarchies and therefore creates opportunities for authentic collaborative learning with colleagues and employees. Furthermore, educational leaders' ability to engage in and model critical self-reflection through research (also referred to as an **inquiry stance**)[2] leads to improvements in school and district culture that have a ripple effect on transparency, collaboration, and relational trust. When you, as a leader, facilitate applied research by creating communities of practice (groups of stakeholders investigating an issue) in your school or district as a central part of sustainable change, the school or district benefits. Not only does the level of professionalism and professional learning improve, but so does the exchange of knowledge and skills.

When you lead through learning and thought partnership, you invite staff members, colleagues, and other educational stakeholders to think and strategize together. Thus, communities of practice are a form of intentional, group-based thought partnership central to effective leadership and applied research. Engaging in applied research within communities of practice that take an inquiry stance on themselves and their organizations empowers you and others to argue against top-down policies and suggest viable alternatives that are based on locally collected and analyzed data. Throughout the book, we conceptualize these communities of practice as the applied research team, which is different from a traditional understanding of such communities. Throughout the rest of the book, we discuss how educational leaders, as members of a team, engage in applied research.

WHAT IS APPLIED RESEARCH?

Applied research refers to research processes that educational leaders can use to address multiple issues in schools and other educational institutions. A primary goal of applied research is to solve **problems of practice** and to support effective engagement in real-world settings. Applied research, which is also referred to as action research, practitioner research, or practitioner action research, involves a series of processes (figure 1.1). Each of these processes is interconnected and informs the others, as indicated by the bidirectional arrows. The processes do not necessarily occur in a sequential order, and they often overlap or occur simultaneously. Although we discuss these processes in depth in chapter 3, we provide a summary here to introduce readers to applied research. This kind of research can use qualitative, quantitative, and mixed methods approaches. In this book, we primarily describe qualitative research processes in combination with preexisting quantitative data because, as the introduction discusses, schools have extensive quantitative data and we believe that the systematic use of qualitative data can greatly improve schools and districts.

Many applied research projects begin with a question, a problem, or another timely topic. A research topic can arise in multiple ways. For example, one middle school principal, Camila, noticed that 12 percent of the students were consistently late to school. To better understand the tardiness, she reached out to teachers she believed might be interested (and have the time) to learn more about this issue. Together, Camila and three teachers at her school met frequently and operated as an applied research team or a community of practice.[3] As figure 1.1 shows, the formation of this team is considered part of applied research. The team worked to understand the causes of the students' lateness and to find out from the students and their families what could help them to be on time. This same problem of tardiness could be developed into a research project in a different way. A leadership team might collectively notice the same issue and decide to collaboratively research this problem as a team. Either way, for this research to be sustainable and valid, there should be more than a couple of people conducting the research. The formation of a group ensures that the research—the work, insights, and recommendations—is done collaboratively.

Once a research team is formed, it collaboratively develops research questions that will be answered by the research. Often, the team members review the existing knowledge about an issue to better understand it and to develop good research questions. This knowledge comes from many sources, such as school-based data and documents, practitioner-generated texts and materials, scholarly literature, prior research, and relevant news and social media. The team should obtain this information and review it throughout the research project and not just at the beginning. The good news is that multiple team members can access and share these sources with the team, thereby cutting down on any one individual's searching and reading time.

After you and your team have developed a set of research questions and reviewed the relevant literature from existing research in these areas, you'll

FIGURE 1.1 Applied research elements

Question or problem
Reflection and action
Research team
Dissemination
Research questions
Learning and collaboration
Write-up
Existing knowledge
Data analysis
Research design
Validity processes
Data collection

design an applied research project that answers your guiding research questions. Many decisions go into applied research design, including the following:

- the type of data that will be collected (e.g., interviews, focus groups, surveys, observational fieldnotes, student work, teacher work, existing quantitative metrics)

- the timeline for collecting data (e.g., a month, a semester, an entire school year)
- the proposed plan for analyzing data (e.g., dividing up data to analyze into manageable chunks, discussing themes that emerge from the data)
- strategies that ensure validity of the research (e.g., having multiple data sources or multiple interviewers)
- who will participate in the research (e.g., what range of constituencies are important to understanding a diversity of experiences and perspectives in relation to the topic)

The choice of **research participants**—the individuals who will be interviewed, observed, or otherwise connected to the data collected for the study—should be discussed as a group. The team should consider the ethical aspects of these choices during the design of the research (see chapter 3 for more details). Data are collected and analyzed as a group, and the themes and findings are discussed in full. Although data collection and analysis are often divided up for the sake of time, the discussions can be structured as professional development sessions. After these sessions, the team presents a summary of the findings in a report or presentation, ideally to the whole community in user-friendly ways. The team then distributes the summary to the relevant stakeholders, who are also invited to help determine action steps in light of the research results.

STORIES FROM THE FIELD

A Superintendent's Approach to Understanding School Discipline

Eleanor is a public school superintendent for a midsize school district. As part of her duties, she is responsible for ten schools and frequently observes and interacts with principals and teachers in these schools. After a year of visiting each school individually, Eleanor wanted to bring the principals of these schools together. She arranged an introductory session in which all principals presented a concern that they were interested in addressing as a group. At this meeting, seven out of the ten principals were concerned about school discipline. One principal worried that some disciplinary policies privileged students from one racial group and targeted others from different racial groups. Another principal had parents and teachers complaining that the school's disciplinary procedures were placing an unfair burden on them, forcing the parents to stay home from work and fill out paperwork and interrupting the teachers' focus on instruction. A third principal said that her school's disciplinary policies were purely punitive, rather than restorative, and thus failed to improve the school's climate and its students' experiences in a meaningful way.

Eleanor was amazed at the principals' different experiences regarding school discipline. She thought that the principals' different experiences provided an excellent opportunity for the principals to work together to learn more about the topic, both in general and as it applied to each school. Eleanor believed that examining this issue across schools would enrich the principals' individual and collective understanding of what issues affected school discipline in their district. Thus, in this example, the problem of practice emerged from the principals' concerns at their schools, and Eleanor realized that having them collaborate would make the research more feasible, broader in scope, and generative.

In consultation with the principals, Eleanor further decided that the principals' professional development sessions for the rest of the year would be related to collectively learning more about school discipline, including policies, practices, and implications. Thus, the ten principals and Eleanor now constituted an applied research team, and together they developed the following guiding research questions: What is the purpose of disciplinary policies and practices at our schools? How do teachers understand and enforce disciplinary procedures? How do students and parents experience school discipline?

To begin to answer these questions, the team members read a few academic articles about school discipline and reviewed the district's and individual schools' policies on discipline. They looked online for trends in various articles about school discipline. They then decided that they wanted to hear the teachers', students', and parents' perceptions of the disciplinary policies and practices in their schools. To narrow the scope of the study, the principals collectively decided to focus on seventh-grade teachers, students, and parents.

They would start with the seventh grade and then take the findings from that study and engage in focus groups in other grades to look for differences or similarities across the various grade levels.

In addition to being a part of the applied research team with Eleanor and the other principals, each school leader developed a research team at their own school to help conduct the research. Eleanor supported the principals' efforts by leading sessions for the faculty and staff, and most principals reported that their teachers were excited about this opportunity. Because the teachers often felt overwhelmed by the logistical, social, and emotional complexities of enforcing disciplinary policies, they were excited to hear that school disciplinary policies were going to change because of the research. The teachers knew that the research would lead to better support for them and their students. Another advantage of this process was that several principals and teachers within the groups had acquired solid research skills in graduate school, and the teams reached out to these people for research training about interviewing techniques, survey development, and data analysis.

This example makes several observations about collaborative learning. It shows how educational leaders, in this case, a group of principals and a superintendent as well as teams of principals and teachers, can work together in applied research. It demonstrates the importance of collaboration and a growth mindset—an approach to life, oneself, and professional practice that approaches problems and other issues as inevitable and, even more so, as opportunities to develop new skills and knowledge.[4] The example also shows the kinds of data that can be generated and shared through applied research. Finally, the example reflects how educators need to collect and analyze qualitative data to make locally relevant decisions about any issues they are addressing. These decisions lead to more effective and holistic approaches to student learning, psychosocial development, capacity building, and professional development in schools and districts.

In the next section, we discuss four mindsets that are important for leaders who wish to use this collaborative applied research approach to support their efforts for sustainable innovation.

LEADERSHIP MINDSETS

Leaders trying to conduct applied research for organizational change need to embrace several mindsets. As described earlier, applied research requires that its leaders have many attentive qualities, such as authentic engagement, broad perspectives, and humility. Leaders in applied research value contextualized, data-based stories as a means to understand and validate local experiences, priorities, and knowledge. To conduct effective applied research, leaders need to adopt and continuously cultivate four mindsets: (1) situating themselves as learners, (2) reconsidering data and research, (3) viewing collaboration as integral to professional excellence and development, and (4) challenging the status quo. The integration of these mindsets can help individuals develop transformative, relational leadership. Let's examine each of these mindsets.

Situating Yourself as a Learner

Leadership scholars distinguish between managerial and transformational leaders. Some leaders act as managers, focusing on tasks without a vision or an intentional road map, and other leaders take a more transformational approach, acting intentionally and with vision to transform their organizations.[5] Leadership approaches in practice are often not so bifurcated; many leaders may combine different elements of managerial and transformational leadership styles.

With a transformational approach, leaders position themselves as learners committed to a mindset of personal and organizational growth. Thus, we recommend that as the leader, you take on the role of learner and do so with intention that is visibly and verbally communicated.

A learner mindset positions leaders as transformational rather than transactional. It enables distributed leadership—where there is a clear leader and where several informal leaders share meaningful work. As models of distributed leadership, communities of practice (or applied research teams) allow for all the individuals in the group to increase their trust in colleagues, their knowledge of the issue, and their professionalism. In this regard, the practice of thinking together as a learning organization becomes embedded in applied research.[6]

To embark on collaborative applied research to drive sustainable change, everyone in the organization must be open to change. They must understand that these changes will be based on research findings rather than instinct or the latest educational trends. As the leader, you need to be explicitly open to change through learning. And you must foster openness in the group by encouraging a culture of risk-taking. This stance embodies what it means to be a learner. Furthermore, you need to understand that innovation can involve failure (the hallmark of a growth mindset) and support this type of learning. In this constructive educational environment, when you become a learner, others do, too. This environment also offers new and exciting leadership roles for educators and ensures that change efforts from applied research are visible, integrated into the organization, and formally appreciated.

Within our approach to applied research, leaders take an inquiry stance, or what some scholars call a learning stance.[7] Leaders continuously look for opportunities to learn, and they approach learning as a regular, active, and central part of work life and professional development.[8] Part of this stance involves admitting that you do not have all the answers and are interested in others' opinions and experiences. Our approach to applied research for sustainable change necessitates that you position yourself as a learner open to change and continuous improvement through research practices. As a learner, or as the "head learner," you open up new possibilities for growth for yourself, your staff members, and, subsequently, the students.[9]

Reconsidering Data and Research

Besides positioning themselves as learners, leaders in applied research for sustainable change must also see research as doable and practical (rather than as an ivory-tower pursuit). Reconsidering what counts as data and research is an important piece of this mindset because the research must be viewed as something that practitioners do collaboratively and routinely. Leaders and their teams should appreciate and understand qualitative data and should cultivate strategies for applied research. We discuss both qualitative data and applied research throughout the book. In this section, we underscore the importance of qualitative research in education.

As mentioned in the introduction, the role of today's educational leader has become increasingly multifaceted and externally driven. US educators are nowadays flooded with numerical data because of federal and state policies and accountability measures.[10] Furthermore, the current top-down policies of high-stakes testing, external assessments, and systems of reward and consequences have an impact on students, teachers, and leaders.[11] Not only do public schools face these pressures, but private schools also need to compete on these national norms as well.

In the current educational environment, quantitative data are privileged over qualitative, and by ignoring the value of qualitative data, educational leaders are missing out on important knowledge that can help them achieve their goals of improved outcomes and experiences for students, teachers, parents, and communities. Of course, **quantitative research** is not the problem. But without an understanding of the various perspectives and experiences of individuals in the setting, decisions based solely on quantitative data can be misguided and even harmful. Furthermore, the data that schools and districts receive (and are evaluated on) tend to stem from state and national policies and are therefore not locally developed. These data are *acontextual*, meaning that they lack the very context that shapes them, and so they are less useful in driving local change. Evidence shows that when it comes to understanding school policies and practices, acontextual data lead to inappropriate or even punitive actions and implementation models. For example, school and district leaders are held accountable for quantitative student progress data and are evaluated solely on their ability to move those numbers. If leaders do not meet these outcomes, the leaders, schools, and districts often face punitive measures. Considering qualitative data in addition to quantitative data would help leaders and organizations have a deeper and more holistic understanding that can drive improvement and help stakeholders make more-informed actions that respect the local context.

School and district leaders are trained to evaluate quantitative data and base decisions on this information, often without careful consideration of any mediating influences on these metrics. Were these leaders and other education professionals given opportunities to build the technical skills necessary to gather and evaluate local qualitative data (combined with existing or collected quantitative data) and build strategies from all this information, they would make better-informed and more-effective decisions. Given these realities, local knowledge production is not only valuable for all school or district stakeholders, but also a necessity. We approach applied research from a systems-thinking approach to foster transformational, sustainable change, and we envision applied research teams in which learning and leadership are shared by everyone affected, including students, teachers, parents, and administrators.[12] A transformational leader understands that site-based research can contribute both to the local organization and to national data and dialogues.

Viewing Collaboration as Integral to Professional Excellence and Development

Another key leadership mindset pertains to the kind of collaboration and professional exchange that we have discussed throughout this chapter. You can support a learning stance for professional reflection by promoting active collaboration in a community of practice.[13] In applied research, these communities of practice constitute teams that collaboratively examine and address problems of practice through conducting valid research. With this form of relational leadership, all the stakeholders improve the organization by collaborating and conducting context-specific applied research on a current issue.[14]

When leaders publicly describe themselves as learners, they enjoy opportunities to hear multiple perspectives, including those of parents, students, teachers, and other community members. Furthermore, collaborative learning communities decentralize expertise in a way that allows room for shared and collective expertise to grow. An ethos of thought partnership is built on a firm belief that everyone is an expert of his or her own experience, that educators develop a wisdom of practice, and that each person therefore has important ideas and experiences to share in a research team.[15] This belief is the basis for the collaborative establishment of group norms around listening to others and keeping an open perspective.

In this sense, the applied research team, as a community of practice, will set group norms and be positioned at the forefront of changing institutional culture and functioning. Even after a first research project is concluded, the team will continue to meet regularly and function as collaborators since the team becomes part of an integrated professional development plan. Then, as new topics surface that would benefit from local research and professional development, the team can decide together how to shape a new research project, examine a new issue, request specific kinds of professional development, and involve other stakeholders. The members also serve as a dissemination team so that there are multiple voices sharing what is happening throughout the research process, as transparency is important for the long-term success of the research project. When this kind of engagement is integrated into professional development and school functioning more broadly, teachers and principals experience an inspiring kind of professionalization that helps them become more intentional about their work and relationships in the workplace. This intentionality raises the level of accountability to each other and builds trust.[16] Thus, a mindset that views collaboration as central to professional development and organizational functioning helps propel applied research for sustainable change.

Challenging the Status Quo

Over several decades, a shift in the educational sector has changed what it means to be a teacher and a leader in the United States. Because of this shift, which is influenced by business-style reforms and national standardization, educators have far less autonomy and control over their work.[17] In some circumstances, when principals do have greater autonomy, there are often incentives that pit principals and teachers against each other.[18] Educators are expected to rely less on professional judgment and cultivated wisdom of practice and to teach and lead with deference to standardized, high-stakes tests.[19] We do not present applied research as a panacea or a singular solution to this decades-long shift in the education sector. However, we do believe that a strong leader can creatively and collaboratively diminish these problems. Applied research emphasizes the intellectual and relational work of educators and creates a greater sense of agency and professionalism. Thus, integrated collaboration can emerge as an antidote to the powerlessness and isolationism so pervading US education these days.

Strong leaders cultivate a mindset that both recognizes and challenges the status quo of contemporary schooling (and society more broadly) in several ways. To understand the various current issues in schools, strong leaders must consider which kinds of data can help contextualize the existing quantitative metrics. They must also work collaboratively with multiple representative stakeholders, seeking out a range of social identities, to understand the issues at hand and to put them in context. Leaders also need to examine schooling holistically and critically, exploring how macro-sociopolitical forces (e.g., testing bias, classism, structural racism, and ideas about language learners) shape schooling, teaching, and learning. Finally, leaders should look beyond aspects of education like test scores and national expectations and consider other aspects that can make schools better and more equitable places for students, educators, and families. In each of these areas, challenging the status quo requires looking at the same settings with new eyes that reflect a more critical understanding of social norms and constructs and how they become instantiated in school settings.

In addition wanting or needing to drive improvement, educational leaders should approach schools as complex social enterprises. At every moment of every day, there is dialogue revelatory of student experience, most of which is missed, ignored, or denied. The thoughts, actions, and opinions of students, teachers, staff, and parents are not the driving force of decisions or changes in most schools, and this omission is even worse in underserved and underresourced schools.[20] By collecting data that pay careful attention to students and adults say (and don't say) and do in your own setting, with a thoughtful eye toward how schools are structured around equity and identity, you can better implement informed and sustainable changes. You'll succeed because you'll better understand the context and the different constituencies, with their range of experiences, resources, logics, and concerns. Finally, by encouraging individuals with different backgrounds and experiences to join applied research teams and by selecting research participants with a range of perspectives, you can bring to the forefront voices not typically not heard.

PRACTICES TO START

To begin leading and conducting applied research for sustainable change, leaders should put into practice the four leadership mindsets just described. Because these practices depend your own role and situation, we suggest customizing and refining them to make them even more relevant to your setting.

PRACTICE 1: *Situating Yourself as a Learner*

As you situate yourself as a learner, you will model, introduce, and convey this mindset to your staff, faculty, board members, parents, and students. We recommend that you transparently and proactively communicate this mindset so as to model this process for others. To model this approach, you frequently communicate your learner stance with others in formal and informal settings by saying seemingly simple phrases such as "I don't know" and "Thank you for teaching me that." You can also announce to your leadership team or your staff that you are working on developing a learning stance and a growth mindset and then invite your colleagues to consider doing the same. By embodying and encouraging this mindset, others will begin to notice and perceive ways that they can also operate as learners.

After modeling a learner mindset and encouraging others to do the same, you can introduce the concept of applied research for sustainable change to your faculty and staff. One way to do this is to share an overview such as in figure 1.1, using Eleanor's experience as an example and then brainstorming with stakeholders what processes they might want to examine in your school or other organization.

As you share your learner mindset with others, we also recommend that you listen carefully to a range of constituency groups to try to understand both the larger and the smaller sociopolitical forces present in every interaction, classroom, and policy. You should focus on issues of structural inequity and intersectional social identities and how they play out in public spaces, including schools and workplaces.[21] You can begin this approach by having the leadership team brainstorm the ways that staff and faculty (as well as students) talk about how social identities shape individuals, groups, and whole-school experiences of teaching, leading, and learning. Try having structured discussions about these social and educational realities, and model what critical listening looks like even when you disagree with what the other person is saying.

PRACTICE 2: *Reconsidering Qualitative Research and Data*

Many professional development sessions in schools and districts are devoted to reviewing quantitative data. During one of these sessions, you could try asking those in attendance what the quantitative data do *not* capture. By discovering these questions, you and the rest of the group could consider other data that would help you better understand the quantitative data and develop a more holistic understanding of the issue at hand and the contexts that shape it.

In addition, you can consider sharing with staff members and colleagues examples of how qualitative data have been used to foster innovation in educational settings. (We include examples throughout the book.) You could then present examples that feature ways that understanding context shapes learning outcomes, student engagement, and faculty learning and development.

Besides giving examples of qualitative research and the importance of context, you could also think about working with colleagues to teach and learn research skills. You might seek out team members who have had exposure to qualitative research design and methods through graduate work (or other means), and have those individuals actively share their knowledge.

PRACTICE 3: *Fostering Collaboration as Integral to Professional Excellence*

To foster a learning community among staff and colleagues, leaders can present themselves as head learners.[22] As a head learner, you embrace personal and professional change and collaboratively address these with your staff and colleagues. You can demonstrate your support for collaborative research teams by incorporating applied research during ongoing professional development. Even though everyone attending structured professional development sessions may not be a part of the research team, the team members can gain alternative perspectives, see how their emerging findings are received, present data at sessions, and work together to brainstorm ideas.

Leaders can diligently foster collaboration between people with different views. You need to seek out dissenters and encourage them to have a role in the applied research, whether they are directly on the research team or are consulted by members of the research team. These practices are connected to the learner mindset that we recommend you model with your colleagues and staff as you teach careful and active listening skills.

As we discuss throughout this chapter, collaboration is central to applied research for sustainable change. In this regard, we recommend that leaders promote and support opportunities for structured collaboration. Such cooperation does not have to be solely related to formal applied research projects. By modeling a learning stance, staff members may feel empowered to take up research themselves. Thus, principals could build in extra time for departments and other groups to work together. Superintendents can bring together principals to discuss common issues as a district and within each school. Time is a precious commodity in schools, but when leaders value something by finding ample time for it, it is more likely to be effective.

You can also send a brief, open-ended (i.e., qualitative) survey to colleagues, principals, or teachers, or all these stakeholders, asking them to prioritize their most pressing professional questions and needs. You can then design a workshop to have individuals strategize and brainstorm ways that these issues could be examined through an applied research approach.

PRACTICE 4: *Challenging the Status Quo*

We encourage leaders to critically consider the habits that have become invisible in their organizations. For example, look at how seats are arranged for professional development sessions and how parent meetings are run. How are teachers evaluated in your schools, and how are students disciplined? What do these practices convey about what is valued in the organization and what is punished and less valued? Aspects of the organizational culture and routines that you notice can then be examined collaboratively with colleagues. We discuss organizational culture in more depth in chapter 2.

Another way to challenge the status quo is to acknowledge how context mediates everything in educational institutions, including schools. Keeping this in mind can help you understand the circumstances that shape individual and group experiences in these institutions. You can then consider collecting qualitative data to support this contextualized approach to leadership, teaching, and learning.

Recognizing how the status quo marginalizes individuals and groups, leaders should be an active, vocal, and thoughtful advocate for marginalized faculty, staff, teachers, students, and parents. Focusing on these experiences, when appropriate, in applied research studies can create significant opportunities for learning and institutional growth. Schooling and education are not neutral; they are part of a larger national history and the current political and social environment. With this in mind, you can use applied research projects to eradicate from your institutions the practices that enforce broader prejudices, deficit orientations, and oppression.[23]

CHAPTER SUMMARY

By supporting the leadership mindsets in this chapter, you can help create an open atmosphere in which ineffective practices can be examined and changed. This chapter introduced the concepts of applied research for sustainable change and leadership through collaboration. We detailed processes involved and included an example of how a superintendent involved ten principals in both a collective applied research project and individual projects at the principals' schools. We discussed four key mindsets that educational leaders should cultivate if they want to engage in applied research for sustainable change:

(1) situating oneself as a learner, (2) reconsidering data and research, (3) viewing collaboration as integral to professional excellence and development, and (4) challenging the status quo. Finally, we conclude with suggestions for how you can begin to cultivate a practice of applied research with your colleagues and others.

TWO

Organizational Culture and Norms in Applied Research

"A GARDENER DOES not begin with nothing, even if planting on a barren field." This metaphor, shared with us by a former principal and superintendent in his twentieth year as an educator, signifies that educational leaders do not begin a new plan or initiative on a barren field or blank slate. Rather, they begin somewhere in the middle of the life of an institution already in motion. To continue the metaphor, gardeners need to understand the conditions of their piece of earth—its existing nutrients (and lack thereof) and its strengths and vulnerabilities—to plant something that can take root and, with proper care, flourish over time. In the field of education, leaders will want to learn about the conditions of the schools and professionals they lead and understand everyone's role in the education ecosystem.

In the service of these goals, this chapter discusses how you can better understand your organizational culture and norms and incorporate applied research studies into the organization's existing policies, practices, and systems. We also share multiple ways to approach these pieces of the school-based research puzzle and to structure studies that consider your organization's mandates and other priorities.

In this chapter, we address the following questions:

- How do leaders assess organizational culture and norms?
- How can leaders cultivate support for applied research?
- How do leaders collaboratively assess organizational values?
- How can leaders consider the ways that organizational culture contributes to applied research projects?
- What strategies can leaders employ to interrupt institutional cultural values and norms that are problematic and that resist change?
- How are institutional mission statements used to initiate and ground applied research projects?

THE ROLE OF CONTEXT AND CULTURE IN SCHOOLS AND APPLIED RESEARCH

Every organization has unique cultures and subcultures. Thus, for educational leaders seeking to support sustainable change, connecting research to existing culture and norms is an important component of any change initiative. Doing so helps you to base applied research on an informed understanding of relevant institutional history. Therefore, to conduct applied research for sustainable change, leaders need to consider whether context and culture, including practices and policies in schools, support research. Furthermore, understanding the values and goals underlying these policies and practices helps leaders design research that is more useful and sustainable. Educational leaders engaging in applied research need to consider important institutional realities. Among these realities are an organization's culture and norms, both individual and school values, organizational mission and vision, formal and informal roles of all stakeholders, and national and school policies. As we discussed in chapter 1, leaders collaborate on applied research teams and collectively consider aspects of organizational culture, priorities, and roles. Thus, we recommend that leaders and teams take three approaches crucial to the sustainability of applied research: assess organizational culture; centralize crucial intersectional concepts of race and identity; and evaluate institutional policies and values.

Assessing Organizational Culture, Norms, and Roles

"Culture eats strategy for breakfast," a statement often casually attributed to management guru Peter Drucker, resonates with organizational leaders because it exemplifies how organizations, and the people within them, function. The leaders with whom we work find this quote useful because it helps them grasp the powerful force of organizational culture and suggests that successful approaches to organizational development attend to local culture as the great mediator of all other aspects of institutional functioning. To lead effectively, leaders must work to understand organizational culture—both its explicit and implicit aspects—as a dynamic, shared set of norms and beliefs that undergird and shape an organization's daily life.[1]

Culture consists of the values, beliefs, underlying assumptions, attitudes, and behaviors shared by a group of people. It is dynamic, not static, and is shared and yet also individually interpreted.[2] The explicit (visual and verbal) components of an organization's culture are noticeable every day at work. Whether you are walking through a hallway, sitting in a classroom, attending a meeting, eating in the lunchroom, or standing on the playground, the organizational culture surrounds you and permeates all aspects of your day-to-day professional life. How people behave, the language or languages used, how decisions are made and shared, the symbols that are meaningful, the stories, and the daily work practices all represent the culture of an organization. Something as seemingly simple as bulletin board content, a newsletter, the interaction of colleagues in meetings, or how people collaborate demonstrates aspects of an organization's culture.[3]

Understanding the multiple, dynamic contexts within an organization, presently and historically, is central to driving sustainable organizational change. Whether you are a leader of students, teachers, principals, or districts, a central focus should include the classroom setting; among other things, you need to pay close attention to what students are learning, how they engage with concepts, and their relationships with peers and adults.[4] As a leader, this entails cultivating your practice of continuously learning the context through frequent and meaningful engagement with different stakeholders, including students, teachers, staff, parents, and colleagues.[5] Additional local aspects for you to consider include verbal and nonverbal communication, group dynamics, people's emotions, and assumptions that otherwise might go unnoticed. Emotions can be particularly informative, as individuals do not tend to get excited, upset, or angry about things that are unimportant to them. Thus, strong emotional reactions are windows into what people care about. For example, try to notice if people seem engaged, excited, agitated, angry, or withdrawn and in what moments or activities. Do they smile and interact with others in meetings? How do they behave as they walk by their classrooms or desks? Similarly, examine how people handle conflicts; keep an eye out for cultural norms and practices.

When you observe and interact with people in the setting, try to watch for what is *not there* or *not said*. For example, if no one mentions something that you think is important (such as student mental health issues as they relate to extreme behaviors), this oversight may indicate missing aspects of the organizational culture. Paying attention to what is *not* said in a discussion can help you understand your organization's culture.[6] For example, are race, gender, culture, and ethnicity discussed when they are relevant to an issue at hand, or are they considered taboo or uncomfortable topics and therefore ignored? These kinds of unspoken attitudes are grounded in larger belief systems that should be excavated and then critically considered. In this sense, these issues are entry points to better-informed decisions and actions.

Posing a series of reflective organization-based questions and working with others to carefully discuss these questions are important steps in this discovery process that we recommend happen before most of the research begins. We suggest beginning by individually (and then collaboratively) considering some of the questions presented in table 2.1 to help you and your group explore what insiders think and feel about the organization and its culture.

The kinds of questions in the table can help you learn more about your organization. Leaders tell us that this kind of context-centered learning is in itself a powerful leadership tool. They believe that this approach of asking a series of critical questions about context enables them to engage with people

TABLE 2.1 Discussion questions to better understand organizational culture

- What major events, relationships, conflicts, and other issues shape institutional micropolitics?
- What values are shared? How widely are they shared, and by whom? How do you know?
- What are the espoused priorities in your setting? Do the espoused priorities match actual practices?
- How do professional groups communicate within the group and between them?
- Is the culture one of trust or mistrust? Of courageous conversations? Of resistance, one-upmanship, or siloed functioning?
- What are the big hot-button issues in your institutional politics and policies? What are the triggering issues in terms of equity, professional development, and team functioning?
- Are counselors and learning specialists viewed as necessary to conversations about student progress? What are the implications of their participation?

in their work setting differently and with more curiosity. It helps these leaders understand that each person has a subjective interpretation of the place that shapes their experiences and performance. Furthermore, it helps bring people together as they agree to take an inquiry stance on themselves, their own practice, and the organization as a whole.

Organizational norms are a central component of institutional culture. People's formal and informal roles are guided by expected norms. These standards guide how individuals act and engage with each other. For example, the practice of raising one's hand to speak in a professional development session reveals an expected norm that is also linked to the organization's culture. Or the expected norm for the role of principal is often to lead professional development sessions. These norms are not universal, and cultures, norms, and roles vary depending on the institutional context. Aspects of these norms may be part of what educational leaders want to change. However, change takes time, and to make change processes sustainable, leaders need to understand how an organization functions underneath its everyday veneer.

Organizational culture, norms, and roles are reflected in both formal and informal policies. Many US schools, like the nation more broadly, embrace a culture of individualism.[7] Another common characteristic of most schools is teachers' reluctance to have observers in their classrooms. This resistance has many causes, including the evaluative nature of most observations (even if they are not intended to be so) instead of a collaborative one. If an educational leader wanted to change this norm so that teachers frequently observe others' classrooms and engage in productive conversations that lead to improvements in practice, other norms would need to change. In this example, the school or district might have formal or informal observational policies in place. A leader would want to be aware of these and ask how these policies could be connected to the research. For example, a leader could invite the leadership team to review the current policies on peer observation. If there are no formal policies, the team could examine the informal ones. This way, before the leader and the rest of the research team begin designing a study related to this issue, they understand the current institutional attitude about observations. Thus, an understanding of the organizational culture and norms becomes central to designing sustainable applied research studies.

The leadership team must also remember to explore norms from a range of institutional perspectives. They should learn about the roles that people officially and unofficially play in communication pathways, including giving and receiving feedback. The team should also examine organizational norms related to disagreements and exchanges of ideas as well as how individuals in the organization respond to formal and informal changes. To help you and your team consider these norms from multiple perspectives, table 2.2 presents useful discussion questions for you to address.

TABLE 2.2 Discussion questions for considering norms from multiple perspectives

- What role do self-governing bodies, like task forces and unions, play?
- In what ways do people view professional development and their own professionalization?
- How are decisions made within the organization? Are these guided by formal or informal norms or policies?
- How are disagreements handled?
- How are colleagues expected to collaborate?
- What norms guide how the organization engages students, families, and communities?
- What is the range of perspectives on these questions?

By hitting the heart of the matter on organizational norms from various perspectives, these questions can help you to assess and then reenvision the norms. Using the information obtained by asking various people in your organization these questions and carefully recording their responses, your research team can explore data related both to your research questions and to the organization as a whole.

As a leader, you have your own understanding of the organization's norms and culture. However, when attempting to make sustainable change, you must intentionally learn about norms from different perspectives. You must seek out these perspectives not just at the beginning of your tenure as leader but also throughout your term because institutional culture changes over time. Finally, it is important that you and your team carefully carry out these tasks because some norms are unspoken or considered out of line with official norms.[8] Related to this, in the next section, we discuss how leaders can prioritize a focus on issues of equality, race, and intersectional identity.

In addition to your organizational culture and norms, your team could consider other aspects of your organization. What roles do people officially and unofficially play in your school or district? How are decisions made, and who is involved (or not) in them? We recommend that you as a leader examine people's formal and informal roles related to communication and feedback and decide if some of these roles need to be shifted.

In addition to these internal organizational roles, leaders also contend with external organizations, trends, and policies. These outside forces may include the involvement of tasks forces and unions as well as formal and informal roles that other organizations have in relationship to your school or district. Furthermore, there are external policies, including the national Every Student Succeeds Act (ESSA), and state and local laws and policies that leaders must be aware of and address. The success of applied research for sustainable change requires leaders to intentionally work to understand multiple dimensions of organizational culture, norms, and roles. Given how busy and stretched educational leaders already are, we approach these processes with an eye toward their feasibility. Leaders can streamline the assessment of external culture and norms in terms of time and resources so that the assessment is not only viewed as possible, but also repositioned as essential.

Focusing on Equity and Identity

As the chief learner, you need to keep in mind that issues of identity and equity, which center around intersections of race, social class, sex, gender, religion, and so on, can trigger people. The most successful and self-aware leaders we work with create a set of working concepts that help them and their colleagues effectively plan for and navigate conversations about topics that can be upsetting or controversial. Understanding concepts such as racial microaggressions, racial literacy, racial stress, and intersectionality can help leaders with conversations and programs involving social identity. In this section, we describe these concepts using the work of Howard Stevenson (our colleague and friend and a thought leader who has applied his theories in public and private independent schools for over three decades) on how these concepts play out and can be applied to equity work in US schools.[9]

Racial microaggressions are common, often brief verbal, behavioral, or environmental indignities, either intentional or unintentional, that regularly communicate racial slights or insults toward people of color.[10] Scholars have adapted this framework to discuss other microaggressions, such as ethnic, cultural, gender, social class, sexual orientation, and religious microaggressions. We recommend that you introduce the concept of microaggressions to your colleagues and staff and discuss real examples of where these affronts might be occurring in school and the rest of your community.

This concept proves useful in helping people identify, communicate, and understand how daily school life affects people from nondominant groups. When individuals are aware of microaggressions and consciously avoid engaging in them, organizations are making their environments less hostile to people of color and other marginalized individuals and groups.

Racial stress occurs when racialized experiences cause psychological, emotional, or physical stress.[11] This definition can be adapted to apply to different kinds of stress, such as pressures related to culture, religion, and sexual identity.

The concept of racial stress helps explain people's physiological responses to conversations or other interactions about race, social class, ethnicity, and other sensitive issues.

When people can determine when they feel racial stress and share this experience with others, they are beginning to develop a practice of racial literacy.[12] *Racial literacy* is the ability to read, recast, and resolve racially stressful encounters.[13] Reading means decoding racial subtexts. Recasting entails reducing stress in racially stressful encounters using racial mindfulness. And resolving involves negotiating racially stressful encounters toward a healthy conclusion. Thus, people with racial literacy can read and experience interactions by monitoring their personal stress and triggers. Racial literacy gives people the coping strategies they can immediately employ if they find themselves stressed or tense during conversations about identity and equity (and then throughout their everyday lives). Leaders need to remember that there are always varying levels of racial literacy, self-awareness, and tolerance for disagreement about these realities and issues.[14]

Intersectionality describes how different forms of identity-based discrimination intersect and interact. The idea is important since people have intersectional identities (e.g., black and female; gay and mixed race; or queer, multi-ethnic, and Jewish) and should be recognized in the complex ways that they self-identify rather than in identity silos.[15] Talking with other educators about their own intersectional identities is a good way to introduce this concept to them, as the discussion offers a starting point for them to consider other people's identities in intersectional ways.

While there is no panacea for handling the stress—your own and others'—that often emerges during conversations about identity and inequity in schools and society, these kinds of conceptual tools of interpretation help you and others create a more open, communicative, and safer emotional environment for discussion. Such an environment can help people feel less helpless and alone and can help prevent or deescalate tensions or heated disagreements. You need to improve your own racial literacy and emotional intelligence to help others do the same. Building and then sustaining a culture that is unafraid to examine issues of social identity and inequity and can do so productively will improve everyone's racial literacy, to the benefit of your school or organization. Through our discussion of safe and brave spaces in chapter 4, we discuss important strategies for helping your team have potentially difficult conversations (see resource A at the back of the book for additional information).

Evaluating Institutional Policies, Mission, Vision, and Values

An organization's values are often reflected informally in its culture. Institutional mission and vision statements can be a formal indication of an organization's values. By collaboratively reviewing these statements early on, an applied research team can begin to build a more complex understanding of existing organizational culture. Broadly, a mission statement is a formal summary of the aims and values of an organization. The statement is an organizational road map that explicates what the organization wants to become and guides transformational initiatives by setting a defined direction for an organization's trajectory. Examining the mission and vision closely can help you learn what the institution expressly values and, conversely, what it does not. In addition, you should think about how your applied research projects support the mission of the institution. Consider also when the mission was written (e.g., ten years ago or last year), who wrote it (e.g., whether teachers, students, and families had input), and how the current stakeholders relate to it.

In our work with school leaders, we find that in many schools and districts, mission or vision statements are often ignored in organizational functioning. For instance, when we ask to see the mission statement at many schools, we are met with blank stares. The mission statement is neither used nor familiar to the people who work there. In many institutions, employees rarely know what the formal mission or vision states. They were not brought onboard with it; nor does it drive their performance appraisals or shape the way they approach their job. Consequently, the mission statement is not viewed as a living document. When people are aware of their organization's mission statement, it is still seldom used as a framework for curriculum, programming, or professional development.

Because of these disconnects between an organization's stated mission and reality, formal, focused discussions of the mission and vision, including what issues or people may have been left out, can be an empowering first step of a larger discovery process. Building on these discussions is a way to start an informed and collaborative change in culture. Still, cultural change takes time, and leaders typically experience resistance when attempting to change the culture of their organizations. In the following section, we suggest ways that you as a leader can overcome resistance to organizational change and applied research. In chapter 3 and beyond, we continue with specifics on how to build these processes into your applied research design.

OVERCOMING RESISTANCE TO ORGANIZATIONAL CHANGE

To overcome the inevitable barriers to change and make applied research less daunting, we recommend several tactics for leaders. First, leaders should pay close attention to the circumstances that contribute to the dynamic nature of organizational culture. Second, they should consider where the research can support the organization's values, as reflected in its mission and vision statements. Finally, leaders should involve many individuals in the research, making sure to include those with different perspectives as well as influential and well-respected individuals.

By paying close attention to contextual factors—including relational dynamics and norms regarding communication and collaboration—that shape institutional culture and subcultures, you can anticipate how potential research findings and changes will be received by various groups within your organization. You and your team can then brainstorm ways to proactively address these concerns and point out how the research supports institutional values. In addition, when leaders align the applied research projects with organizational mission and vision statements, naysayers lose their arguments, and the research is more likely to succeed. Finally, by involving key stakeholders and other influential members of the institution and deliberately including vocal dissenters, you increase the likelihood that the findings will be well received. At the end of this chapter, we include practices to help you strategically approach organizational change.

In the following section, we present an example. We look at how Vance, the head of a school, overcame faculty resistance to pedagogical change (as well as resistance to him in general as a new leader) at his high school. Vance employed a number of the strategies discussed here to cocreate the most ideal conditions possible for his faculty to become more open to change and, further, to view themselves as change agents.

STORIES FROM THE FIELD
Overcoming Resistance to Engender Organizational Change

Vance, who is a second-year head of an independent high school in the Midwest, was concerned by how resistant the faculty were to new ideas and initiatives. A common refrain after an exciting professional development meeting (that most faculty members seemed to enjoy) was this: "That is a great idea, but it just wouldn't work here." Other faculty members made comments along the lines of "Our students, and especially their parents, would not be receptive to changing that. It's the way it has always been; it's tradition." Faculty members' concerns were varied. They worried that if they stopped assigning copious amounts of homework, parents would think the teachers were not being rigorous enough. Some teachers thought that shifting to a more inquiry-based approach in their classrooms would diminish their authority and would hurt their students' learning and competitiveness in the college admissions process.

Vance decided to take an approach that required the faculty to critically examine their teaching and their relationships with students rather than assuming that their current practices were just fine. Thus, before Vance could even begin an applied research project with faculty, he needed to overcome their resistance to change. This resistance was related both to the teachers' suspicion of Vance because he was new to the school and to their reluctance to try new pedagogical strategies.

To address this issue, Vance recruited some highly respected members of the faculty—including several who were typically naysayers to new ideas—for leadership positions on the schoolwide research team. Of course, just putting these seven individuals on his inaugural team did not make them suddenly open to change. Thus, to slowly involve them in a new process, Vance began with a review of the school's mission and vision statements. Among other steps, he asked the team members to read through the statements and write down what they thought stood out, what was missing, and what questions or concerns they had. The team then had an in-depth discussion about what they noticed in the statements and where they thought the school achieved its mission. They also discussed areas where the school could improve. This initial discussion led to an even more focused conversation about what steps could be taken to address the identified areas of concern. This conversation resulted in a shared discovery that both good and bad aspects of their institutional culture—such as the lack of trust, the sharing of professional challenges, and peer mentoring—developed from years-long politics and experiences with performance appraisals.

Through this discussion, Vance learned that the teachers saw performance appraisals as an unhelpful and dispiriting outgrowth of a years-long deficit orientation (an attitude that focuses on what a person is presumed to lack) rather than as a means of supporting professional and personal development around areas of needed growth. Vance, in his second year as head of the school, had already begun to realize that the appraisal system seemed like an artifact of a time when only the head's opinion of a teacher's performance mattered (rather than inviting peer assessment). By carefully listening to the teachers describe the evaluation process, he learned how the attitude of the prior head, who viewed the teachers as truly subordinate and less knowledgeable, shaped the culture of the school as well. These insights helped Vance position himself as a leader who wanted to revive and reinvent a system of appraisal that teachers would feel reflected a more holistic view of their knowledge and skills. He worked closely with two key colleagues to create a task force that could present performance appraisal models at the following meeting. During that meeting, Vance, the task force, and the applied research team members decided on two options to present to the rest of the faculty for review.

Vance was a part of these discussions, but the faculty drove the process. His belief was that starting with something so important and charged for the teachers, giving them space to make decisions on something that affected each directly, and then selecting a new system of teacher evaluation recommended by the teachers for the teachers would show clearly that he intended to take action from applied research going forward.

Vance took this issue-embedded approach within the broader revision of the mission for many reasons. It constituted a quick win on an integral aspect of organizational culture. Furthermore, given that this issue had persisted for so long, the intentional inclusion of veteran and new teachers and staff members enabled an intergenerational approach that brought distant faculty members together when faculty cohesion had been an ongoing concern. Vance felt strongly that most of the current faculty at the school were genuinely committed to ensuring students' holistic success, which he knew needed to be reflected more fully in the mission and vision statements and in the appraisal system. After the careful review of the mission and vision statements, the faculty decided to draft new ones that would be vetted by faculty, staff, and a select group of students. They worked across two meetings, with a task force of team members working in between, to rewrite and codify the new statements. These statements were then shared across all stakeholder groups, such as staff, faculty, administration, parents, students, and community members, as a part of a revival of energy and communication between groups in and beyond the school. In addition, the new mission and vision statements were used to frame the introduction of the new appraisal system.

As mentioned, the revisions of the mission and vision statements are examples of quick wins (or, rather, multiple quick wins) that enabled a strong and collaborative beginning for an applied research team. That an immediate and longer-term change happened through visible collaboration is a sign of Vance's own vision of the institution he leads. The great transparency of the process helped people begin to trust Vance and want to follow his lead, when up to then, trust in the head of the school had been a problem for some faculty members. Furthermore, the openness set the stage for Vance's more organic, interconnected approach to teaching, learning, and leading. His engagement with the faculty made clear that he was not autocratic or punitive like his predecessor. It also showed that he believed that teachers should have a say in their own professional development since they know what they need best. Thus, Vance created a set of communities of practice within the larger applied research team to focus on specific topics and then to assemble as one large inquiry community to explore and discuss solutions together. Doing so created more energy, curiosity, and humility and opened up critical inquiry in a way that allowed for even more faculty and staff energy to surface and be directed toward positive, constructive institutional progress.

After all this excitement, the revision of the school's mission spawned another question. The research team decided it had to learn more about how the school conceptualized and promoted holistic student success—meaning academic, social, civic, and psychological well-being. The team members believed that exploring and understanding this issue together would help them actualize the revised mission and vision statements, which began with the declaration "We are actively committed to the holistic development of our students."

Vance and his research team, with the help of a select group of student leaders, designed and conducted a brief applied research study to explore how students, teachers, staff (e.g., coaches and counselors), and school board members define student success. The goal was to learn enough to collaboratively consider how to deepen and widen these stakeholder groups' view of academic and athletic success. From Vance's perspective, this research was urgent, given that national quantitative data showed that on average, the school had a much greater number of significant stress-related mental health issues than did its independent-school peers. To help his faculty and staff understand where he was coming from, Vance showed them how the statistics compared with their peer schools. Shocked to see how much worse their school's ratings were, the teachers and staff felt prompted to take action on behalf of their students. The research began with a great focus on learning from a range of stakeholder groups about these issues and their experiences with them. The entire process of defining success took only three weeks, with the allotted time coming from free periods, prep periods, lunch, and professional development time.

This research proved productive and fascinating as well as troubling. After conducting what they called "flash interviews and focus groups," the research team found that teachers and students alike narrowly defined success, though in different ways. Broadly, teachers exclusively defined student success as high grades, a respectful attitude, and in-class engagement. Students defined success largely as social standing, athletic performance, and grades. Neither group seemed to consider things like emotional intelligence, humility, perserverance in the face of struggle, the ability to collaborate, or empathy as key factors of student success, even though mainstream research shows that these qualities are considered predictors of lifelong success.[16] The disparity between the students' definitions of success and those of the teachers opened up multiple discussions, which happened largely in focus groups led by research team members during the advisory period. The discussions pointed to some of the more harmful perspectives on student socialization and development.

Vance demonstrated a sophisticated understanding of the culture and subcultures at his school. This understanding helped him and his research team to strategically structure applied research that then began to shift the institutional culture. By wisely including influential faculty members from different departments and representing different subgroups, such as veteran and new teachers, the research recommendations were better received. And as mentioned, Vance actively recruited some of the most vocal individuals who seemed the most resistant to his ideas. These resistors deepened, rather than derailed, the learning. Because Vance structured the applied research team and its early actions as a response to a shared problem voiced by teachers, the process felt responsive to their needs and positioned it for success. Vance also ensured that the findings were immediately useful to the teachers, staff, and students. Finally, he took a multistage approach to change and, in doing so, connected multiple policy, practice, and pedagogy dots in a way that felt less overwhelming because they had developed organically.

PRACTICES TO START

Before beginning an applied research project, leaders and applied research team members need to develop a solid working understanding of their organization. In this section, we discuss ways for leaders to examine their organization's culture, values, mission, and structure. To do so, we describe how two practices, focus walks and flash focus groups, can be adapted to reveal multiple aspects of an organization. We also present questions to help you guide discussions of these topics with colleagues during professional development sessions, faculty meetings, and other interactions. We encourage you to adapt these strategies and topics to your own situations and to select the topics that are most relevant to you and your organization. In addition to these two practices, we also present a useful framework for discussing crucial concepts. Many leaders have found the framework helpful when they are engaging their colleagues in sometimes difficult conversations.

PRACTICE 5: *Focus Walks*

One way to observe the cultural aspects of your organization is to take walks around the building or buildings to observe some of the physical signs and signals of organizational culture, values, and policies. If you are observing a school, you may find that students and teachers are useful guides on these focus walks, because as you and the guides walk around together, they can narrate, answer your questions, and actively show you how they see the school. If you are observing district culture, think about the different stakeholders who could serve as a guide or who could accompany you on these walks. For example, you could ask a parent to walk through the school or district office with you or ask a teacher to go to a school board or city council meeting with you. It is important to make a note of what people from various stakeholder groups focus on or ignore during these walks. Leaders and others can take focus walks frequently to observe organizational culture in action. Resource B presents sample questions to keep in mind during a focus walk. The questions concern an organization's environment, physical space, or communication norms and can be adapted to the setting of the walk.

PRACTICE 6: *Flash Focus Groups (Small-Group Discussions)*

Flash focus groups are brief gatherings of small groups of people whom the research team asks a series of questions. These discussions are often first held with members of the applied research team and then with other stakeholder groups. We recommend including people who will speak their minds and who will listen carefully to other people's thoughts. Many leaders have the research team members decide on the groups of stakeholders. Before each session, decide on several questions that you'll ask the group, and have a clear goal about what you want to learn. During the sessions, we recommend having two team members present so that one member can take detailed notes. Flash focus groups should comprise around five or six people. The sessions should last between twenty and thirty minutes; you will probably be able to ask only a few questions so that all individuals can respond. In resource C, we list potential questions that are grouped according to topic (culture, mission and vision, priorities, policies and systems, and organizational structures).

CHAPTER SUMMARY

A goal of this chapter was to help educational leaders assess the important roles of context, culture, norms, values, and policies in their organizations. Understanding organizational culture can help you anticipate barriers to change and design applied research projects that are more relevant, collaborative, and sustainable. The chapter presented several practices that leaders can use to examine aspects of their organization. It also detailed an example of a school leader who overcame resistance to organizational change by engaging the relevant stakeholders on his applied research team in the co-construction of a new institutional mission, vision, and appraisal system. By better understanding the culture and subcultures of your organization, you can design better collaborative applied research for sustainable change. The design of this research is the topic of the next chapter.

THREE

Designing Applied Research

THIS CHAPTER DISCUSSES how leaders and their teams can design effective and actionable applied research. We describe important research design considerations, including research goals, actionable research questions, existing knowledge about salient issues, strategic data collection and analysis methods, the right mix of participants, the validity of the study, the allocation of time and resources, and how applied research drives informed action. We also discuss the importance of designing research that is flexible, rigorous, and systematic, and we explain how to design applied research projects that agree with organizational goals and that put existing metrics and data in context. This chapter presents an example of an assistant principal who bases a study on a variety of existing data sources in schools. We also show how a head of school made time for an applied research study by making it a part of her accreditation process. The chapter concludes with practices to help leaders and teams begin designing their own applied research projects.

We consider the following questions throughout this chapter:

- What is research design?
- What processes are involved, and how can you develop these?
- How can you address ethical considerations in your research design?
- How can you plan for validity in the research?

- How can you best utilize existing school or district data in applied research projects?
- How do leaders make time for efficient and actionable projects?

WHAT IS RESEARCH DESIGN?

The term *research design* refers to the way that researchers plan and set up a research study. Applied research is not linear or sequential, and accordingly, its processes do not necessarily occur at discrete stages. However, you should have an idea of what you want to study and have a research team assembled before you begin to plan your research. There are several important considerations related to applied research design (figure 3.1). Let's now delve into these considerations in detail.

DETERMINING YOUR RESEARCH TOPIC AND GOALS

What are you studying? Your ability to clearly and succinctly answer this question is important to designing an applied research project. There is no end to potential research topics. You may be interested in how faithfully teachers implement curricula. You may want to investigate students' attention span on standardized tests. Or you may want to look at administration structure, parental issues, or community support. And the list can go on. The point is that you want to have a clearly defined research topic, and because you are working with a team, this step may require multiple meetings in which you and the team discuss and agree on a research topic. This collaboration is vitally important so that the focus and goals are clear and shared among team members.

One way to help focus a team is to brainstorm about the goals of the research. What are you and the team hoping to accomplish through the research? Each of you may have personal, professional, intellectual, or practical goals or some combination of all these.[1] Research goals and objectives refer to why a study is important and what the researchers hope to accomplish. Thus, we recommend that research teams individually and collectively consider their hopes

FIGURE 3.1   Research design components

Research topic and goals
- What are you studying?
- Why are you studying it?
- Why is it important?

Research methods
- What methods will you use to answer your questions?
- How will you sequence these methods?

Existing knowledge
- What is already known about the topic?

Research questions
- What questions are you trying to answer through your research?

Participants
- Who will be involved in the research study?

Validity
- How are you planning your study so that it is as rigorous and valid as possible?

Time and resources
- What resources, including time, are required to complete this research?
- Have you created a timeline?

Action potential
- Where do you see potential changes stemming from this research?

Research design components

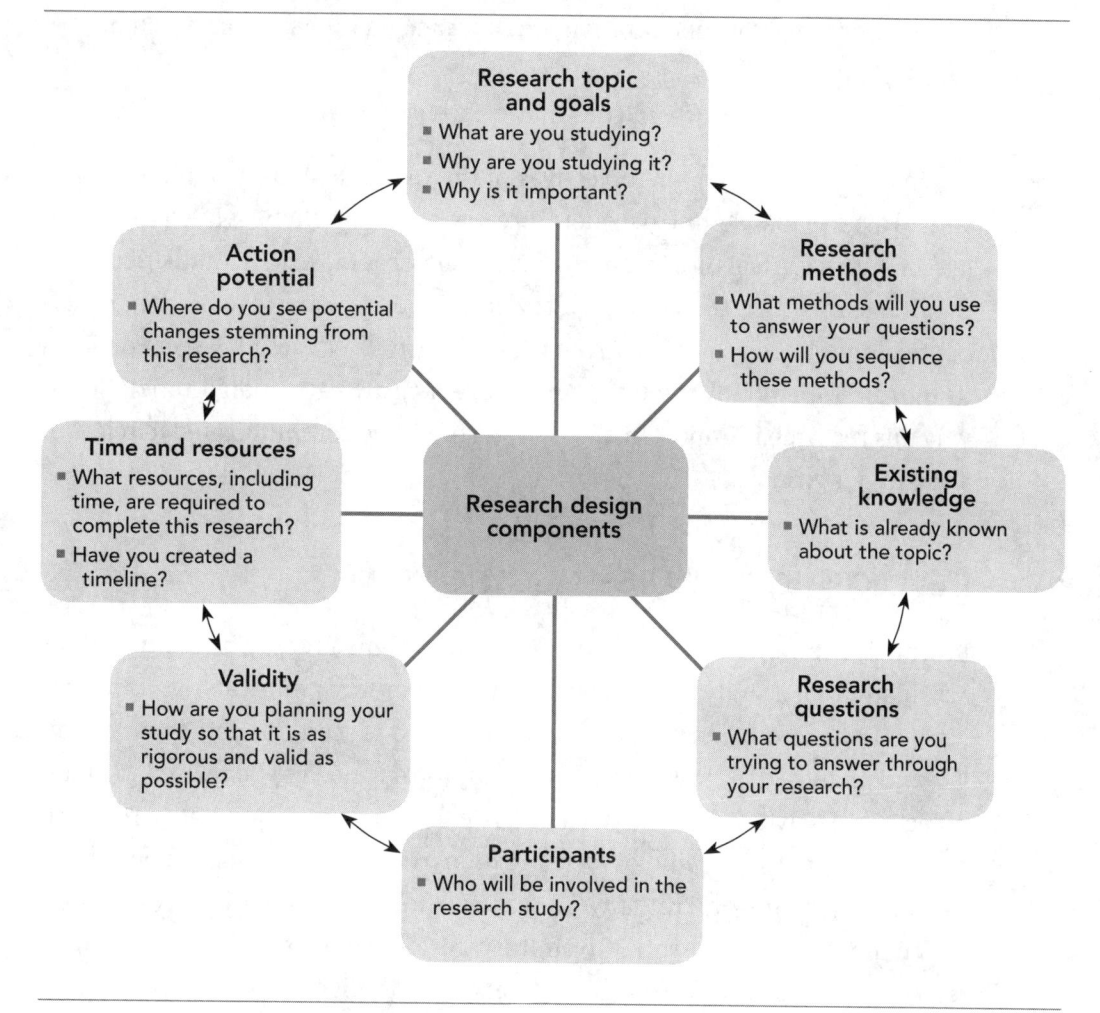

for this research and why these expectations matter on an individual and organizational level. Applied research goals depend on many factors, and teams often have multiple goals. Some common applied research goals include the following:

- understanding the value and effects of a program or an intervention
- improving students' academic performance

- developing students' critical thinking skills
- improving the collaboration among teachers in their departmental groups
- assessing the pros and cons of the parent resource center

In applied research, the objectives of the research should be directly relevant to a particular setting. Furthermore, the goals should be related to a problem of practice, that is, a site-specific (e.g., a classroom, school, or district) issue that the team wants to better understand and for which the team then develops evidence-based solutions. Even though these objectives may seem obvious to the team members, the team must have a clearly articulated rationale for why this research is important and why it should be communicated to relevant stakeholder groups.

DEVELOPING RESEARCH QUESTIONS

Research questions are central to research design. Broadly, these questions articulate what a study attempts to understand or learn more about.[2] Developing qualitative research questions is an iterative process. As you begin to collect and analyze data, your research questions may need to be revised to better reflect the newly acquired knowledge.[3] The fluid nature of qualitative research questions signals the value of focusing on participants' everyday experiences. In contrast, in most quantitative research studies, the research questions do not change during fieldwork. Given the goals of applied educational research, research questions should be as customized and reflective of phenomena and experiences in the setting as possible. While research questions may be refined over time, all research designs should begin with guiding research questions, and in some cases, these questions do not change. At the research design stage, the research questions help teams decide what they want to learn more about and the best ways to answer those questions.

Qualitative research doesn't aim to generalize to a broad population. Rather, it attempts to focus on one population and learn deeply about those people's experiences. Qualitative research is so well suited for school and district work because it helps generate information about the local texture and complexity in relation to broader trends and issues. The researchers explore how local circumstances influence the issues being studied. In your applied research, you answer questions focusing on your own situation to understand the range of experiences related to the topic. Thus, one way to develop qualitative research questions is to be specific to the realities within your setting.

Take the following research question: How do eighth-grade teachers determine if students are ready for ninth grade? You could not answer this question using applied research, because you cannot generalize for all eighth-grade teachers. However, you can answer a question about the eighth-grade teachers at your school and how these specific teachers determine ninth-grade readiness and its relationship to eighth-grade curricula. Thus, researchable research questions could be as follows: How do the eighth-grade teachers at Jackson School understand what it means for students to be ready for ninth grade? What factors do these teachers use to make these readiness decisions, and how are these factors incorporated into eighth-grade curricula? In table 3.1, we

TABLE 3.1 Tips for developing applied research questions

TIP	EXAMPLE RESEARCH QUESTIONS
Be specific.	■ How do eleventh-grade students at Presley High School prepare for standardized tests? How do these students' perspectives about standardized test preparation vary?
Ask about people's experiences, perspectives, and processes.	■ How do first-year teachers in the Mayview School District experience the district's induction program? What are the teachers' perspectives about the skills they are developing or not developing? ■ What are fourth graders' experiences with project-based assessments at Carver Elementary School? What have these students learned about content from these assessments?
Keep questions free from assumptions and judgments; word questions as neutrally as possible.	■ Assumptive question: How can teacher fidelity to the tenth-grade English curriculum be improved? ■ Neutral question: How faithful are tenth-grade teachers to the public English curriculum in Texas? What are these teachers' experiences in implementing this curriculum? What circumstances affect the teachers' fidelity?

present additional tips to help you develop researchable questions as well as examples of research questions.

When you are developing research questions, a common challenge is conflating your research questions with the goals of your study.[4] Research questions can help you achieve your goals, but study goals do not tend to directly translate into researchable questions. For example, a goal of your research might be to reduce student suspensions. Thus, to reduce suspensions, you first have to learn more about them. Here is an example of effective research questions related to this issue: Why do teachers at Rosemont Charter School suspend students? How do students at the school experience being suspended? What, if anything, do they believe they learn from these suspensions? As we discuss in the next section, identifying the existing knowledge about an issue is central to research design and can help you formulate specific and researchable questions.

There is a difference between research questions and interview questions. Research questions are the primary questions that drive the *entire* study. Interview questions are those you ask participants (e.g., during an interview) as you collect data for your study. We discuss interview questions in detail in chapter 5. Finally, although a study can have more than one guiding research question, we caution against having too many research questions, as the scope of the study can become too large. Of course, the number of questions depends on the topic, the study goals, and the context, but anywhere from one to three questions is typically considered a reasonable number. Usually, there is one main question and then one or two supporting questions that are all related to the topic.

EXAMINING EXISTING KNOWLEDGE

Understanding what is already known about a topic is an important part of all research. In applied research, this step includes reviewing the existing scholarly literature and considering other forms of existing knowledge, including data already collected, institutional missions, educational policies, and ideas from popular culture and the media. Depending on your research topic and goals, you may want to consider several areas of existing knowledge. As figure 3.2 illustrates, these areas include the following sources:

- scholarly literature, which broadly refers to theoretical and **empirical** (research-based) studies
- popular culture and the news media
- local settings such as communities, districts, schools, and classrooms
- local data from the multiple data sources present in a school or district (e.g., student assessment data, student and teacher attendance numbers, enrollment information, demographic data, mission and vision statements, policies, curricula, graduation rates, local community norms, school environment information, parent involvement information)

FIGURE 3.2 Sources of existing knowledge

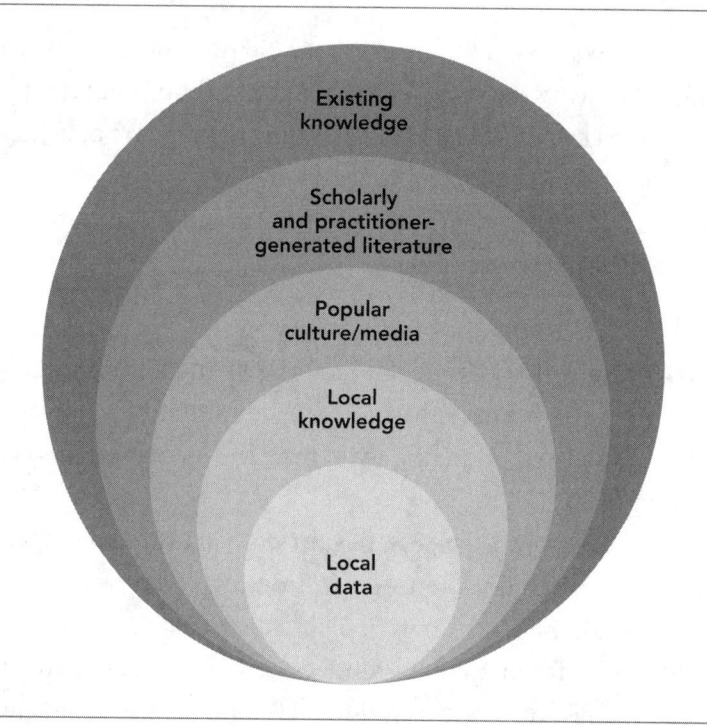

- Existing knowledge
- Scholarly and practitioner-generated literature
- Popular culture/media
- Local knowledge
- Local data

A grasp of the existing knowledge will help you and your research team design your applied research study. Because there are multiple sources to consider, you could divide the work among the team members. One group could review the scholarly literature; another could review media articles and popular culture sources; another could gather district information, policies, and data; and another group could consider school-related policies and data. Each group would need to find and compile multiple sources. To find scholarly and practitioner-generated literature, for example, you could use Google Scholar to search key words and could search scholarly databases (e.g., JSTOR). Another way to find such literature is by asking other individuals, such as faculty at a local school of education and state or district personnel. As team members skim articles for relevance, we recommend also looking at bibliographies to see which scholars and articles seem to be frequently cited; the team should then also review these articles. It can be helpful to keep a few questions, such as the following, in mind as you read the literature:

- What is the context of the text? Where did the study take place? Who conducted the research, and what are the authors' affiliations?
- What is the key argument that the text is making? What evidence do the authors use to support this argument?
- What questions or concerns do you have about the argument?
- What are the relevant takeaways from the article or research for your team?

After reviewing their assigned sources of existing knowledge, each group should present to the entire research team a summary of what they have learned. After this presentation, the team members may decide to revise their research questions.

In the earlier example of a research team studying student suspensions, the team revised its research questions to focus on the seventh- and eighth-grade students, because after a review of school and district data, the team found that students were more frequently suspended in these grades. Thus, the team's revised research questions were as follows: Why do seventh- and eighth-grade teachers at Rosemont Charter School suspend students? How do seventh- and eighth-grade students at the school experience being suspended? What, if anything, do they believe they learn from these suspensions?

During your review of existing knowledge, you and your team may discover a large quantity of district- and school-related information, including policies, reports, and numerical data, about whatever issue you are addressing. Thus, you may decide to continue reviewing the existing data as a part of your research methods. At the end of this chapter, we describe how to write an *existing-knowledge memo*: an additional way for teams to summarize and incorporate already-existing information into their research design.

Building on Preexisting Data and Metrics with Applied Research

Schools, school districts, and other educational organizations are replete with many kinds of data that are used for a range of (albeit limited) purposes.[5] In table 3.2, we have adapted and updated a list of educational data that James "Torch" Lytle, professor, veteran educational leader, and former superintendent, principal, and teacher, developed many years ago. You can use the data already in place in your school or district to develop a more holistic, informed, and relevant applied research project.

Surprisingly and unfortunately, the data that we've just mentioned have been put to limited use or no use at all, either because people do not know how to make this information actionable or because they do not consider it a source for learning about issues that concern them. In other instances, staff will sometimes only briefly review data to write a required report. Considering preexisting educational data in combination with the data you collect is part of what makes applied research projects integrated and sustainable. In this way, the review of data becomes less perfunctory and more connected to the life of an educational organization. Although you could skip a review of preexisting data for your applied research, the goal is for you and your team to answer your research questions holistically, taking many perspectives of the questions into account. For this reason, reviewing a variety of data sources can help you better understand a topic and determine what data you still need to collect.

TABLE 3.2 Examples of preexisting educational data

Student data	
▪ Demographics ▪ Enrollment and attendance records ▪ Report cards, progress reports ▪ Discipline records ▪ Student assignments (e.g., classwork, homework) ▪ Standardized test scores ▪ Individualized Educational Plan (IEP) data ▪ English language learners' proficiency scores	▪ Percentage of students on free and reduced-price lunch ▪ Participation in Advanced Placement and International Baccalaureate coursework and in career and technical education programs ▪ Percentage of students on track to graduate ▪ Transportation services eligibility ▪ Students' emergency contact information

Employee data	
▪ Personnel files and payroll ▪ Attendance records ▪ Demographics	▪ Teacher grade books, observations, and lesson plans ▪ Teacher credentials, certifications, and evaluations

School data	
▪ Curriculum materials and grading policies ▪ Code of conduct; mission and vision statements; handbooks ▪ School media: website, yearbooks, alumni material ▪ High school graduation rates ▪ Physical environment ▪ Faculty meeting agenda and minutes ▪ School budget and expenditure records	▪ Teaching and student schedules (e.g., teacher planning time, student ability grouping); student-to-teacher ratio ▪ Counseling and nurses' office records ▪ Parent or guardian attendance at events ▪ School surveys ▪ Preexisting action research studies

Organization or district data	
▪ Administrative and board meeting agenda and minutes ▪ Operating, categorical (designated for a specific purpose), and capital fund budgets ▪ Program evaluations ▪ Union contracts and grievance decisions	▪ Census block or school catchment areas ▪ Attendance records ▪ College matriculation and retention rates ▪ Mission and vision statements; district website

Source: Adapted from James Lytle, "Public School and School District Data Sources," unpublished handout, 2008.

What you do with preexisting data depends on the research questions that guide your study. In the following section, we discuss an example of an applied research design that a team developed after reviewing student assessment data.

STORIES FROM THE FIELD
Designing an Applied Research Study According to Preexisting Data

Charles is an assistant principal of a K–8 public school in a large urban district. He noticed that students' reading scores on standardized tests had plateaued over the previous five years. This lack of progress was of particular concern to Charles, given that the school's mission was to develop scholars who could participate in, and contribute to, the academic and professional world in an increasingly competitive global environment. As a result, Charles decided to investigate the literacy instruction throughout the school. He told the principal that he would like to design an applied research project to help him and the school better understand the issue. Charles began by assembling an applied research team, which consisted of three teachers, the school reading specialist, a parent representative from the home and school association, and the district's literacy coach. The team met after school once a week, as that was the only time all of them could meet. Charles and the principal were able to give each team member a small stipend for participating in this work. Before deciding who might be interested in serving on this team, Charles and the school principal developed a list of individuals who could help represent multiple perspectives on the team.

The team's first task, after an introductory meeting in which the topic, goals, and processes were overviewed, was to assemble a variety of data sources to examine together. At this first meeting after the introductory one, the team members identified the following preexisting data sources that related to the goals of their action research:

- Standardized test scores from the last five years, to identify specific areas of strength and areas of needed growth

- Textbooks and other curricular documents from each grade, to identify how literacy instruction was already built into the curriculum and how it could be integrated and emphasized
- Two weeks' worth of all the teachers' reading lesson plans, to examine the current classroom routines and pedagogical strategies that could be tweaked to incorporate literacy instruction
- Samples of passages that students were required to read in each subject area, to understand what was expected of students in terms of their reading in different subject areas (e.g., vocabulary and syntax)
- Samples of writing assignments and student responses from each subject area and any rubrics used to assess the assignments, to understand what was expected of students in terms of writing in the different subject areas (e.g., vocabulary, spelling, and grammar)
- Students' portfolios that focused on their literacy development over the first half of the school year

Charles asked the school's administrative assistants to assemble several packets composed of these strategically selected data sources to be shared with team members before the third meeting.

During the second meeting, after collectively reviewing and discussing the assembled data sources, the team members revisited their goals and decided on the other sources of existing knowledge that they would engage to further develop the research plan. Among other sources, they would seek empirical and theoretical research pertaining to literacy instruction, test outcomes, and student achievement. Each team member would also speak informally with two colleagues to get their impressions of the issue. The goal was to take a quick pulse of the situation, to get a range of opinions, and to begin to make the research public. The members decided that each person on the team would also read one academic article and one practice-based source (such as a curated teacher blog or practitioner publication) and return for the fourth meeting ready to move forward into the inquiry.

At the fourth meeting, everyone shared what they had learned from their reading, their discussions with colleagues, and the connections they had made between the reading and the preexisting data sources that they had reviewed. From this deep level of initial inquiry, people were excited about the topic, realized its importance, and together decided that they needed to narrow their topic, create clear goals for their collaboration, develop focused research questions, and determine how they were going to collect additional data to answer their research questions. Deciding that the goal for their work together was to improve reading scores in all the tested grades, the team developed the following guiding research questions:

- What is our school's approach to literacy instruction?
- How does (if it does) this approach vary according to grade levels and teachers?
- According to teachers, students, and the assessment data, what areas of literacy should our school prioritize?

The members spent the rest of this meeting reviewing the preexisting data in relation to their newly established research questions and goals. They noted both their excitement and their concerns. Notes were taken at this and every meeting. These notes were saved and could be used as data. Given all these data sources, the group decided to create a password-protected Dropbox to house all the individual and collective work, process documents (meeting minutes, agendas, etc.), and the preexisting data. As we discuss in depth in chapter 6, this kind of intentional data organization and management is extremely important to the research process. This also includes notes on the articles and texts that each person shared with the group during the meeting.

At the next team meeting, the members settled on the additional data they would collect and developed a timeline for their research. They wanted to understand their approach to literacy instruction and then develop a strategy that they could have in place by the beginning of the following school year. During the three scheduled professional developments days at the end of the present school year and before summer break began, they could introduce their plan to the entire school. The team used this already-scheduled professional development session as a deadline for the work. They worked backward to plan the team meetings to ensure that the members would be ready to introduce their strategy to the school by these dates. Thus, as a part of the design process, they mapped out a specific timeline so that they knew they would have ample time not only to collect the data, but also to analyze them and create output in the form of a report, a set of action steps, and so on.

The group spent two months collecting data. It held focus groups with students to have them reflect on their experiences in reading classes, and the group conducted interviews with teachers to learn more about their approaches to teaching literacy. In addition, the team members interviewed each other in pairs to further document what they learned in their group meetings as well as their own approaches to literacy instruction. Data collection also included observational fieldnotes wherein each team member visited a classroom and took notes about concrete examples of literacy practices in action. Finally, Charles and the other team members asked all the teachers to respond to the following questions via email: "What are your guiding beliefs about literacy instruction? How are these beliefs reflected in your practice? Please explain your answer with a specific example."

This example demonstrates how Charles and the rest of his team used multiple sources of preexisting data to guide an applied research study and to collect additional qualitative data to help them better achieve their goal of developing a shared vision and practice of literacy instruction across the school. In chapter 5, which discusses data collection, we continue to discuss this example and further detail how the team collected data.

CHOOSING AND SEQUENCING RESEARCH METHODS

Once you and your research team have determined a topic, reviewed the existing knowledge, and developed research questions, you can examine which methods will best help you answer your questions. We discuss these methods in detail in chapter 5 but will touch on them briefly here. In addition to selecting the methods you will use, you also need to consider the sequencing (or order) of these methods. For example, if interviews and fieldnotes are the methods you are using to answer your research questions, you might consider if one method should be implemented first to inform the other method. In this case, you and your research team would consider if conducting observations first would help the team develop more focused and useful interview questions. Conversely, you and your team may also consider if conducting interviews first would help you determine what to focus on in your observations. Importantly, there are no right or wrong sequences in your methods. You and your team members need to carefully consider which methods and sequences will best answer your research questions.

As you choose which methods you will use to answer your research questions, you will also want to consider what permissions will be needed for each method. For example, schools and districts often have research review boards that approve research projects. In addition, before you conduct an interview with a participant, you will need to obtain permission from him or her to conduct and audio-record or video-record the interview. These permission processes are broadly referred to as **informed consent and assent** procedures. Researchers need to inform participants about the research goals, how the data will be used, and how the data will be protected and inform them that participation is voluntary *before* the participants consent to participate in the study.

Informed consent procedures are designed to protect the participants and give them a full and informed understanding of what their participation in the study entails (e.g., how much time it will take, how many meetings they will attend, the duration of project). The procedures also ensure that the participants know how their information will be used and protected, and that they can withdraw from the study at any time. To this end, the research team should also consider and plan for how they will protect individuals' privacy. At a school, for example, it may be easy to identify someone even if names are not used, and the team should make sure that participants are aware of this potential lack of **anonymity** before they agree to participate in a study. We detail additional ethical issues in table 3.3 to help you and your team think carefully about these concerns and the protection of your participants.

Finally, as your team decides on methods, your plan for how you will collect, organize, and store data is an important part of your research design. For example, you might decide that the data will be audio-recorded and then transcribed. If data are recorded, they can be turned into transcripts that are used in data analysis. Transcribing interviews can be a time-consuming and expensive process. Some researchers use notes instead of transcripts, but notes are less reliable. An interview or observation does not become data until it is captured in some way, either in the form of an interview transcript, interview notes, or fieldnotes. The decisions regarding the use of transcripts or notes is related to the research questions of the study as well as practical considerations such as time and resources. In chapter 6, we present strategies for using transcripts, taking notes from audio-recordings, and other analysis processes. The research questions, along with practical and logistical constraints, should guide your decisions on the amount of data that will be collected, who will be included in the study, and how the data will be captured and stored.

SELECTING STUDY PARTICIPANTS

In addition to deciding on your research methods, you and your research team will select the participants in the study. The procedures for determining who will be asked to take part in a study are often referred to as **sampling**. In a majority of qualitative research studies, researchers use *purposeful* sampling: the participants are selected for specific reasons, or selection criteria. For example, if you are studying why seventh- and eighth-grade teachers in a district suspend students, one selection criterion would be that some participants are teachers of these grades in the specified district. You would also include student and parent participants. The specific group of students and parents selected would be related to your research questions.

Thus, in qualitative research, you are selecting participants for specific criteria, which may include personal characteristics, roles, experiences, and

TABLE 3.3　Ethical principles and considerations

ETHICAL PRINCIPLE	DESCRIPTION	CONSIDERATIONS
Minimizing risks and doing no harm	▪ Potential harm to participants from applied research includes psychological distress, social consequences, and lack of confidentiality or anonymity.*	▪ What are the risks to the study participants? ▪ How can the risks be minimized?
Ensuring informed consent and assent	▪ Participants have a full understanding of what their study participation entails and are aware of potential risks (i.e., they consent to participate in the study). ▪ Students and other minors have a full understanding of the study and agree to participate (i.e., they assent to participate in the study). In addition to the assent of minors, parental consent is also required. ▪ Researchers need to obtain verbal or written consent in which the participants acknowledge that they agree to participate in the study and understand the risks.	▪ Are the expectations communicated clearly to the participants? ▪ Are the assent forms worded in an age-appropriate way for students or other minors? ▪ Are the participants aware of any potential risks before they agree to participate?
Protecting privacy	▪ Safeguards should be taken to ensure confidentiality to protect participants' privacy. This issue becomes especially important in small settings, where privacy is a more difficult ethical and professional issue, because anonymity is harder to maintain in a small group.	▪ How are data protected? ▪ What are you promising the participants about privacy? ▪ What steps do you need to take to keep those promises?
Making sure the research is voluntary and not evaluative	▪ Participants should feel that there are no repercussions for declining to participate in a study or for withdrawing from a study later. It must be made clear that participation is voluntary and the study is not evaluative.	▪ Do you assure prospective participants that there are no consequences for not participating in, or for withdrawing from, the study? ▪ How are you ensuring that people trust this promise?
Attending to power issues and asymmetries	▪ Issues of power imbalances and hierarchy must be addressed in research planning and implementation.	▪ Have you discussed power and hierarchy issues in team building and research? ▪ How can you better address these issues? ▪ Is there a "pecking order" in your group or at your institution? ▪ How can the team members feel that everyone's contribution is equally appreciated?

(continued)

TABLE 3.3 Ethical principles and considerations (continued)

ETHICAL PRINCIPLE	DESCRIPTION	CONSIDERATIONS
Attending to dual roles	■ In practice-based research, people must be made aware of the dual and changing roles of a practitioner researcher.	■ How has the leader set the stage for staff and students to understand the nonevaluative nature of the research? ■ How do people on the team reinforce this understanding?
Ensuring transparency	■ The team must be honest about research goals and how the data are being understood and used.	■ Are you keeping people informed about the research and how it will be used? ■ Do people have a designated person and place to ask questions and share concerns?
Being nonjudgmental and respectful	■ The team must be clear that the research is not evaluative and must demonstrate respect for participants.	■ Are you training the team to understand bias and be nonjudgmental?

*Jim Parsons, "An Introduction/Review of Action Research and Its Ethical Practices," *Canadian Journal for Teacher Research* (May 30, 2017), www.teacherresearch.ca/detail/post/an-introductionreview-of-action-research-and-its-ethical-practices.

knowledge; involvement with affinity or interest associations; and membership in underrepresented groups. Personal characteristics may include social identities (race, gender, social class, sex, ethnicity, etc.) and other aspects of people's intersectional identities (since everyone's identities are shaped by multiple factors and dimensions).[6] Thus, when designing a research study, you and your research team deliberately consider how individuals with different identities are included in your study.

Participants may also be selected because of their formal or informal roles. Roles can be professional, social, or relational (e.g., teacher, counselor, principal, student, sibling, mentor). Individuals may also be included in a study because they have had a certain experience. For example, someone may have been a student or a teacher in a specific class or is moving to a school as a transfer student. You might also select participants for their specialized knowledge. The study might need, for example, a guidance counselor's specialized knowledge of the high school application processes. Individuals from different interest groups or from local community groups may also be selected as participants. Finally, when selecting participants in a study, you want to make sure you are including groups of individuals who may typically be underrepresented at your school, district, or institution. These may include marginalized groups or individuals from minority backgrounds. It is essential to have as many voices as possible represented in your research, and purposeful sampling is one way that you can deliberately achieve this diversity.

There is often overlap between all these designations. Without doubt, the intersectional nature of all identities affects people's experiences and perspectives. We nevertheless included the preceding categories to provide examples of why people might be included in an applied research study.

There are no right or wrong reasons for selecting participants, but there should be a clearly articulated rationale for why these individuals are being included in the study. The goal should always be to include a range of individuals with different experiences. Unlike quantitative research studies, the samples in qualitative studies tend not to be representative of the public. However, researchers, through purposeful sampling, thoughtfully consider who is included or excluded from a study and why.

PLANNING FOR VALIDITY

For qualitative research, a valid study faithfully represents the participants' experiences by being intentional and rigorous throughout the process.[7] When designing a research study, you want it to be as valid as possible, given that the findings will inform the organization's program development and other actions and decisions. There are multiple ways that you can help ensure that your data are as accurate as possible. In this section, we discuss four validity-ensuring processes: (1) participant validation; (2) multiple perspectives and data sources; (3) critical reflection on your role as the researcher; and (4) **dialogic engagement**, that is, engaging with others as you make research decisions.

In participant validation, you check in with participants throughout a study to make sure you are accurately understanding, interpreting, and representing their experiences.[8] One way that such participant validation has worked well with applied research projects is for research teams to schedule group check-ins at three distinct phases throughout the research. At these check-ins, research team members invite the participants to a thirty-minute discussion in which the members briefly summarize the data they have gathered so far and invite feedback from the participants.

Another validity-ensuring step is to deliberately include multiple perspectives and data sources in your study. In this way, you as a researcher are making sure that different voices are not excluded from your study and that as many perspectives as possible are included in the research. Different perspectives can also come from the use of different data sources to answer your research questions. You and your team can examine quantitative data in addition to qualitative, use interview and observational research methods, and look for additional sources of already-existing data that can be used in your study.

As an additional strategy for research validity, you need to critically and systematically monitor how you, as the researcher, influence aspects of the research. You then need to monitor your impact so that it does not deliberately bias the research. These processes of regular self-reflection are broadly referred to as reflexivity, which we discuss in more depth in chapter 5.

Finally, dialogic engagement is important in valid and rigorous studies. In dialogic engagement, you deliberately structure your discussions to encourage others, including research team members, to challenge your methods and interpretations.[9] In research design, dialogic engagement involves planning for times when your research team will critically discuss and challenge aspects of the research process, including your choice of research methods, instrument questions, and analytical findings. In chapters 5 and 6, we suggest ways for you and your research team to engage in these critical discussions. For example, once you have collected a few pieces of data from an interview, we recommend that your team discuss how your interview instrument is helping you answer your research questions and if the interview questions—or the research questions themselves—need to be refined.

Validity is not a final product that you achieve; it is instead a continuous approach. Thus, at the design phase, you need to think about how you will plan for and structure validity processes into your research design and then ensure that these processes happen. For example, in your research design, you want to build in opportunities for you and your research team members to reflect individually and collaboratively on the research process and on the data being collected. The objective of applied research is to foster change that will improve individuals' lives and experiences. Thus, researchers must make sure that the investigation is as valid as possible.

ALLOCATING TIME AND RESOURCES

To be successful, applied research projects need to be supported. At the design phase, you must make sure that you and the other research team members will have time to devote to this work. How much time is needed will depend on the situation. As a leader, you may need to consider, among other ideas, additional compensation for staff, release time for teachers, or including the research as part of an already-scheduled professional development session for faculty and staff. The more that applied research becomes an established part of your organization and practice, the more successful it will be.

As an educational leader, you will also want to find time to make applied research a priority and to fit it into your own daily practice. In our previous work in schools and with educational leaders, we found that the success of these projects tends to be contingent on a leader's involvement and support.[10] We understand that it is probably not possible for you to be involved in every aspect of the research; this is why it is crucial to have an applied research team that shares accountability for the project. Table 3.4 summarizes important questions for you to consider.

TABLE 3.4 Considerations for supporting applied research

- How are you, as a leader, prioritizing this research?
- How is the research aligned with your priorities, professional development, and the institution's key policies and objectives?
- Do the research team members have the time they need to devote to this research? If not, how can you help secure this time for them?
- How is the rest of your organization informed about the research? How has your team created buy-in?
- What opportunities are in place for members of your broader staff and community to give input on the research?

Creating a Research Timeline

An important and often overlooked aspect of research design is a realistic timeline for conducting the research. This timeline should detail the dates when you and your research team will complete different parts of the research. For example, when will data collection be complete? What different validity processes will you incorporate, and when will you plan to implement these? In addition to setting deadlines for data collection, you will want to plan for when you will complete the data analysis. Your timeline should also include details for disseminating the research and planning for action. Applied research takes time, considering the busy lives of individuals and the requirements placed on organizations, the team should include flexibility in a realistic timeline. In addition, school vacations, in-service days, conference days, and the like, should be incorporated into the timeline. In the aforementioned example of Charles and his team at a K–8 public school, the timeline they created was based on an already-scheduled event (professional development days at the end of the school year) that the team used as a target date. They planned for the different parts of the research to be ready by this date so that they could share their findings with their colleagues at this event.

Making Time for, and Saving Time with, Applied Research

Connecting the research to everyday activities and deliberately ensuring that research time supports the school or district's existing mission, professional development, and overall organizational improvement can help your organization make time for applied research. As you well know, a common concern among leaders is finding the time—for yourself and your staff—to conduct research.[11] There are several ways to help ensure that the work is doable, efficient, successful, and viewed as worthwhile by faculty and other stakeholders. The most direct and holistic approach is to incorporate applied research into whole-school professional development sessions, both those focused on learning to conduct applied research as a community of practice and those focused on the themes that emerge from the applied research projects. Professional development sessions can focus on themes that the applied research has identified as gaps, learning opportunities, and the like.

Applied research requires that you, as the leader, ensure that faculty and staff members have ample time to devote to this work. You also want to make the work highly visible and valuable, so that those involved in it grow professionally. As a principal, for example, you might give teachers additional release time to devote to the applied research projects, and you might hold professional development sessions dedicated to the research. As a superintendent, you can demonstrate your support for the research by dedicating time for staff members to conduct the applied research projects; you could also incorporate the research into district- or school-based professional development. In any case, professional development time could—and we argue should—be allocated to these processes in productive, efficient ways.

As an educational leader, you want to be directly involved in the research in a way that makes sense. Time constraints will always be an issue for this type of work.[12] As a result, you'll want to clearly commit to this work as an integrated part of your leadership. To help ensure this commitment, you can establish structures that hold you and everyone else on the team accountable. These structures can include monthly meetings with supervisors or colleagues to discuss the research, planned professional development sessions, and research team meetings with predetermined goals. In the following section, we share a brief example from an independent-school leader who made efficient use of time by having research teams collect and analyze the data necessary for the school's accreditation.

> **STORIES FROM THE FIELD**
>
> Double-Traction Possibilities with Applied Research and School Accreditation

Reima, the head of an independent school, had been dreading a stressful school accreditation process. She decided to take an approach that not only made preparing for the school audit considerably less stressful (to her and her staff) but also made it more of an integrated and shared learning process that benefited the school community.

Reima worked with her assistant head to assemble a team that could design and conduct an applied research project to explore two key areas of the accreditation: school culture and student support. These two areas were central to the success of the school's accreditation and the school's overall mission and environment. Reima knew that understanding these aspects of the school's functioning and environment would require a distributed learning approach to the research. The team would need to hear a range of perspectives from a cross-section of constituencies, including staff, students, parents, board members, and the like. Given that the applied research used various research methods, such as focus groups, interviews, and open-ended surveys given to all relevant stakeholder groups, Reima believed that their accreditation report would be rigorous.

To form the research team, Reima and her assistant head selected six teachers who represented different grades and subjects (and different informal social groups of teachers); two students from each grade, representing different social identity groups; the school counselor; and two recent alumni interested in research. Reima and the assistant head worked to achieve buy-in from the beginning by making the applied research project public in the school newsletter as well as on the school's Twitter, Instagram, and Facebook pages. The two leaders shared ongoing knowledge and updates in subsequent staff meetings. In an open (but confidential) portal for teachers and a second one for students, the leaders could share thoughts about school culture and student support. Importantly, two of the teachers were chosen because they had knowledge of action research and were excited to act as informal facilitators and trainers during the first few team meetings. All the teachers were given additional release time to support their work on the applied research.

The team was off and running quickly. The members were asked to keep the school leadership team abreast of all they were learning in brief weekly reports, and they were given templates on which they could fill key insights that mapped onto the criteria for both accreditation themes. Reima took the accreditation process, what most leaders view as a procedural constraint, and transformed it into a meaningful experience and an opportunity to really focus on these vital issues in depth. The knowledge gained about school culture and support for students informed both the school's accreditation and the topics for faculty professional development about school culture and student supports. The knowledge also highlighted areas in which the school was already doing a good job.

As this example shows, for any applied research project to be successful and sustainable, it should be prioritized by educational leaders and connected to the daily life of an organization. Reima and her team continued to conduct applied research after the accreditation was over, and the structures that she had put in place ensured that she and the school had time devoted to this work and the learning that resulted from it. Thus, applied research that is integrated into the life of an institution can be a vehicle for continuous improvement.

PLANNING FOR INFORMED ACTION

As a researcher, you should not assume that you know the answer to a question or an issue before you have done the research. This mindset involves remaining open to learning from the research so that the acquired knowledge can help an organization make informed change and action. While you remain open to different possibilities and answers, it can be helpful at the design phase to think about spaces in a school or another organization that have good potential for change. For example, if you are a math department chair and you know that your principal is considering revising the math curriculum, designing research that would directly inform this potential change can be especially important. Or if you are researching seventh- and eighth-grade student suspensions, you can share this information with colleagues to think about how broader changes could result from your research. Thus, thinking about potential places that are primed for action can help make your research more relevant and effective. In turn, this approach also inspires staff and team members to be more invested in the research when they see that it has a serious potential to lead to change.

Another aspect related to action involves envisioning the different audiences for the research. Are you primarily presenting to your faculty, to the parent body, to education board members, or to students, or to a mix of these groups? Often, you will present your research to multiple audiences. However, you want to keep in mind which audiences you need support from so that you can implement changes. For this reason, at the research design phase, you will consider what questions these individuals would ask of your research, and you then design your study so that it answers those questions. In this way, you are also proactively thinking about potential challenges that the team must anticipate regarding action. Considering these challenges at the beginning and throughout a study (as opposed to at the end of a study, which is more typically the case) can help you design a more successful applied research study.

BALANCING STRUCTURE AND EMERGENT DESIGN

In qualitative research, research processes are iterative, meaning that they can change and evolve throughout a study.[13] Thus, to plan for research that involves qualitative data, leaders should consider the role of **emergent design**, which reflects the fluid nature of research, while still planning for a systematic study.

Researchers who understand emergent design are responsive to everyday circumstances in schools and districts rather than feeling pressured to adhere to a formal academic-style study process. An emergent-design approach to applied research recognizes how the research often changes throughout the process. In turn, planning for the emergent nature of applied research helps make this research as relevant and responsive to daily realities, constraints, and possibilities as possible. In other spheres, these fluid processes are similar to the concept of design thinking, in which creative solutions are applied to solve problems.[14]

Applied research can benefit from both creative strategies and systematic ones. The thoughtful and systematic collection and analysis of data is what makes applied research rigorous and valid.[15] Despite the importance of emergent design in applied research, systematic processes must also guide the research. Applied research systematically addresses the design processes discussed throughout this chapter: developing research goals and research questions, understanding existing knowledge, determining relevant research methods, selecting participants, considering validity, allocating time and resources, and thinking about potential action steps.

PRACTICES TO START

In this section, we present three practices to help you and your research team members design an applied research study. These practices include collaboratively writing a topic-exploration memo and an existing-knowledge memo and systematically addressing research design considerations in an applied research design template (table 3.5).

PRACTICE 7: *Topic-Exploration Memo*

Your goal with this memo, which should be no more than one page, is to collaboratively create a succinct document that details your emerging research topic. Potential questions to address in the memo include the following:

- What are you interested in studying?
- How do you define your topic?
- Why is this topic important in general and to the school, district, or other institution?
- What do you hope to learn from this study?

TABLE 3.5 Applied research design considerations

Research topic and goals	
▪ What is the research topic? ▪ Why is this topic important?	▪ What goals are related to the research? ▪ What are the primary goals of the research?

Research questions	
▪ What are the guiding research questions for the study? ▪ How do the research questions reflect the goals of the study?	▪ Are the research questions clear?

Existing knowledge	
▪ What do I and the rest of the research team already know about the topic? ▪ What literature and theories will we review to better understand the topic?	▪ What existing documents, data, or other resources will we use?

Connection to preexisting data, missions, and policies	
▪ Does the study stem from, or inform, preexisting data? If so, which data, and how? ▪ Does the study connect to the school or institutional mission? If so, how?	▪ How does the research align with organizational culture and values?

Research methods	
▪ What data collection methods does our team plan to use? ▪ What permissions (e.g., approval from school or district research board, consent forms) are needed to collect data? ▪ How will the data be recorded? For example, will interviews be audio-recorded and transcribed?	▪ How will these methods be sequenced? ▪ How will the data be stored and organized? ▪ How will we analyze the data early on to inform the later parts of our study?

Participants	
▪ Who will be included as participants in the study? ▪ Why will we choose these people? Why not others?	▪ How will our team protect the participants' privacy?

Validity	
▪ How will the research design answer the call for validity? ▪ How will our research team ensure that our findings are as accurate as possible?	▪ How can we challenge interpretations throughout the research?

(continued)

TABLE 3.5 Applied research design considerations *(continued)*

Time and other resources	
▪ How will this study be best accomplished? ▪ What resources, including time, are needed to ensure its success? ▪ How can I make myself and the team accountable for this research?	▪ How can the research be incorporated into preexisting structures (e.g., professional development)?
Action plans	
▪ Where does our research team see the potential for action? ▪ Who are the different audiences for the research?	▪ What potential challenges do we anticipate with respect to taking action?
Timeline	
▪ What is the timeline for conducting the research? ▪ When will data collection be complete? ▪ Have we built in enough time to refine our methods and to check in with participants?	▪ What is the timeline for data analysis? For presenting our findings? For developing action plans?

- How do you see this research benefiting the school, district, or other institution?

Each person on the research team should write a memo and have it vetted by one or two colleagues to receive feedback and learn more about how others make sense of what you are planning to study. The members should then discuss the memos with the rest of the research team.

PRACTICE 8: *Existing-Knowledge Memo*

A memo can be written as a team, or individuals could write their own memos and share them with team members to consolidate the memos into a single summarizing memo. A goal of this memo is to reflect on what is already known about a topic from multiple sources, including the school, district, or organization; educational theory and research; and popular culture and the news media. An addition goal of this memo is to present a theoretical summary of your research topic. To write this memo, you will think about what existing knowledge informs your study. This information may include formal theoretical and empirical studies and preexisting knowledge at the research setting, such as policies, quantitative metrics, and missions.

We recommend that you begin this memo by briefly overviewing your research topic and goals by asking yourself and the rest of the team a few questions:

- What do you already know about the topic?
- How is this topic represented in the scholarly and practice-based literature? In your response, discuss at least two or three scholarly and practitioner sources.
- What other evidence informs this topic? Examples of additional evidence might include school mission statements, program objectives, correspondences, evaluation frameworks, and a range of test and assessment scores. Summarize these data, and discuss how they bear on your research.
- What relevant contextual information about the research setting (where the research takes place) or the research topic informs the research?
- What lingering questions do you still have?

PRACTICE 9: *Applied Research Design Template*

To ensure that the research is approached systematically, you and the rest of the team should collectively discuss and document the important aspects of the applied research design discussed in this chapter. We have created a matrix to help you with these design considerations (table 3.5). Your team should work collaboratively to make sure that you discuss all the questions presented in the table, and then you can ultimately fill in the template, found in resource D, with your responses.

CHAPTER SUMMARY

This chapter described important applied research design considerations, including the research topic and goals, effective research questions, existing knowledge, methods, selection of participants, validity, allocation of time and resources, timelines, informed action, and flexibility. We also detailed essential ethical considerations that leaders and research teams should actively consider and plan for as well as ways that you can align your applied research with existing data sources. The examples presented in this chapter demonstrate how leaders connected their research to preexisting data and ultimately saved time by connecting applied research to other aspects of an institution. The chapter concluded with three practices to guide leaders and teams through the design of sustainable applied research studies.

FOUR

Creating Collaborative Research Teams

COLLABORATION IS A LARGE PART of what makes applied research powerful and sustainable. Nevertheless, with collaboration also comes the need to navigate issues of power and group dynamics. This chapter presents ways for you as a leader to strategically recruit and include many people and perspectives on your applied research teams and to proactively address common challenges when forming, working in, and facilitating teams.

In this chapter, we delve into how to assemble a research team that can successfully carry out the applied research processes discussed in the previous chapter. The chapter describes attitudes that help your team function productively, including active respect for multiple perspectives, a commitment to shared learning, and an openness to change. We also detail how capacity building is important to the success of applied research and to your role as a thought and action leader. We share suggestions for forming teams and facilitating teamwork, including how to make sure individuals are aware of, and fully committed to, clear goals, roles, and norms. In an example, a director of curriculum for a charter school network manages an applied research team with varying perspectives. We conclude the chapter by suggesting practices for you to develop reflexivity (reflection on how you as a researcher influence the research) and trust among your team members by engaging them in a structured process in which all of you consider your biases and blind spots.

Throughout this chapter, we address the following questions:

- How can you approach applied research teams as a primary form of professional development?
- What are the central processes and actions for productive collaborative inquiry?
- What are applied research teams, and why are they important?
- How can teams ensure that everyone is aligned on the goals, roles, and norms for the collaborative work?
- How can individuals learn about how their biases and blind spots shape their work?
- How can leaders help others to value, seek out, and navigate multiple perspectives?
- How can you cocreate brave spaces with your research team?

ATTITUDES THAT BUILD COLLABORATIVE RESEARCH

In chapter 1, we detail leadership mindsets central to conducting applied research for sustainable change; these include situating yourself as a learner, reconsidering data and research, viewing collaboration as integral to professional development, and challenging the status quo. Part of what makes our approach different from other organizational approaches to change is, in fact, our focus on collaboration—the very foundation of a successful applied research team. For a research team to be effective and its work to be sustainable, you and other leaders and team members need to develop several important habits, including these: (1) seeking out and learning from multiple perspectives, (2) a commitment to shared learning through collaborative research, and (3) an openness to change.

The Value of Multiple Perspectives

Education influences, and is influenced by, many interconnected factors. Figure 4.1 illustrates just some of the different factors at play in education in the

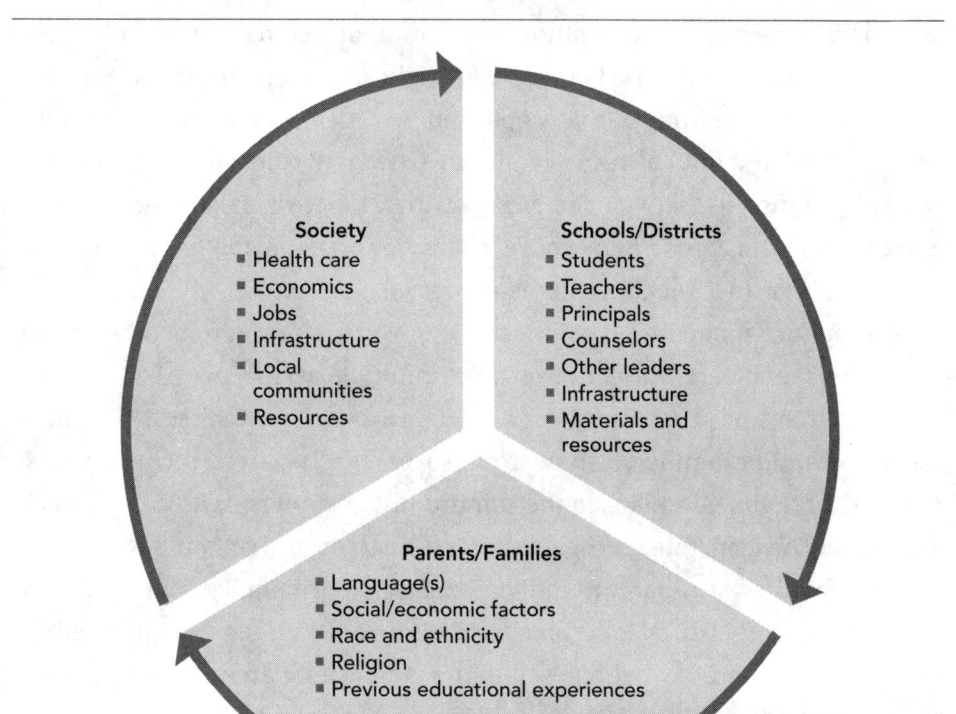

FIGURE 4.1 The interconnected nature of education

Society
- Health care
- Economics
- Jobs
- Infrastructure
- Local communities
- Resources

Schools/Districts
- Students
- Teachers
- Principals
- Counselors
- Other leaders
- Infrastructure
- Materials and resources

Parents/Families
- Language(s)
- Social/economic factors
- Race and ethnicity
- Religion
- Previous educational experiences

United States. These influences come from the school or district, parents and families, and society in general. When working to make sustainable change in education, leaders and their teams need to acknowledge that educational issues are complex, interconnected, and shaped by multiple experiences, realities, and perspectives. To be truly collaborative, research teams must value and engage with these diverse perspectives.

When the team members value the diversity of all their organization's stakeholders—be they administrators, parents, youth, or other members of a community—they recognize that everyone is an expert of their own experience.[1] Every person holds knowledge and wisdom; these qualities are not the exclusive property of those who have formal education, are conventionally considered articulate, have institutional power, or can recite the most recent intellectual trend or theory. Because all people are experts on themselves and make their own meaning of the people and world around them, their insights and perspective should be respected. You will want to cultivate this fundamental, active stance so that you can engage with a range of stakeholder perspectives. Without this broad perspective, change efforts may fail because they do not represent actual people's experiences, needs, or wants.

To conduct applied research for sustainable change, team members reach out to all stakeholders and learn from these multiple perspectives. For example, if a research team is examining low attendance at parent-teacher conferences, the team would examine this issue from several perspectives, including those of the parents and guardians in the community, even those who are not easily accessible. The team must recognize the different forms that families take (e.g., blended families, two-parent families, single-parent families, extended-family child-rearing, LGBTQIA [lesbian, gay, bisexual, transgender, questioning/queer, intersex, and asexual/allies] families, and foster parents) and intentionally recruit participants to include a variety of family and parent perspectives. By listening to these different voices, the team can better learn why some families do not attend parent-teacher conferences. For example, the team might learn that some parents were at work or lacked child care for younger children. The team could then help the school try to address these concerns by offering conferences at different times and providing child care instead of lamenting low attendance. This example shows how seeking out various perspectives in applied research can lead to practical, effective actions that improve educational outcomes. In all these situations, you need to situate yourself as a learner and, as the next section discusses, commit to actively learning through applied research.

Shared Learning Through Collaborative Research

One tenet of adult and student learning is that most of us learn best by trying out and doing something as a part of the learning process.[2] This pedagogical concept of learning by doing is called *experiential learning* and is an important dimension of learning for research teams. In applied research, team members learn about an issue by conducting research. Learning through research is an important process for applied research because the research that we propose largely involves qualitative data and necessitates active engagement with many groups of individuals connected to the topic. Furthermore, the research team members collaborate to design, implement, and assess their research to learn about a topic. Thus, at the heart of this process is learning by doing. This type of learning also entails a commitment, similar to a learner stance, to refrain from assuming you have all the answers and to continuously learn with and from others. In this way, we define applied research teams as communities of practice composed of multiple educational stakeholders coming together to engage in systematic and intentional inquiry to research an issue and develop research-based, customized solutions.

For example, a group of third-grade teachers at an urban elementary school was working together as an applied research team to address what the teachers perceived to be negative behaviors, including talking back to teachers, not paying attention during lessons, arguing with other students, and disrupting class. The teachers sought out multiple perspectives, including students, parents, extracurricular personnel, and community members, to help them better understand student behavior. By collecting data from their students and other stakeholder groups, the research team learned more about student behavior and identified misunderstandings on the part of teachers and students. For example, one misunderstanding lay in how the teachers perceived the students' frequent habit of leaving their seats to sharpen their pencils or get something from their backpacks. The teachers interpreted these behaviors as inattentive and disrespectful. But after talking with students and families, the teachers learned more about the daily realities that shaped these behaviors. In so doing, the teachers realized that they were negatively framing these behaviors, which sometimes reflected the students' needs for short breaks to do these kinds of necessary tasks. The teachers then reframed their understanding of the behavior and clearly communicated their expectations during different parts of lessons. One such expectation was that the students would use the newly instituted "flash breaks" for pencil sharpening and item retrieval.

This example offers a few important lessons, including the idea that we cannot learn about student behavioral issues without talking to students. As this example shows, applied research requires a commitment to reflective learning through an inquiry stance. To conduct this research, you and your team members cannot think that you know best or have all the answers. Everyone will need to engage in active learning and reflection through research.

Openness to Change

In addition to committing to learn through research, applied research teams will want to cultivate an openness to change. For the team to be open to new answers or to interpreting data in new ways, team members are not afraid to be wrong, and they consider different ways of thinking about issues. Humans tend to resist change, even when changes might benefit us. Thus, leaders will want to clearly explain what openness to change and new ideas means. For example, Vance, the head of an independent high school (see chapter 2), deliberately selected members of his applied research team who were both more and less open to change. Thus, part of Vance's role as an educational leader is to help cultivate this openness to change in his research team members. However, it can also be beneficial to select team members who already demonstrate an openness to change so that they can help engage others in this approach.

As the next section discusses, part of your role as a leader is to develop new capacities in your team members (as you simultaneously honor their existing knowledge and capacities). A significant part of building capacity involves helping your staff feel safe enough to take risks. Thus, if you ask your team members and other staff to be open to change, you will want to ensure that appropriate supports are in place to make that openness possible. A favorite quote of one of the superintendents with whom we work is "Change must be open to change." This idea helps remind people not to get too attached to certain beliefs and behaviors so that new possibilities can develop.

CAPACITY BUILDING AS A LEADERSHIP STANCE

As an educational leader, you may play a more or less central role in the applied research team, depending on the topic, the stage in the process, and the strengths of the team. Regardless of your direct or indirect role, you are engaging in an important aspect of leadership, which is developing the capacity of others. In this regard, you are developing the capacity of your staff and colleagues to help improve your organization, with the ultimate goal of improving educational experiences for students. The kind of capacity building that we suggest also serves as a form of reciprocal accountability, in which leaders develop the capacity of individuals to accomplish shared goals.[3] Since accountability is a key aspect of successful teams, sharing the accountability for the success of the applied research process as well as the organization is an important part of leading effective teams.[4] For example, Eleanor, the public school superintendent we described in chapter 1, builds the capacity of her principals to develop reciprocal accountability for improving educational outcomes through applied research. Each of the principals whom she worked with was in turn able to develop the capacity of their staff and, in doing so, also developed a sense of shared accountability. Thus, resource-oriented capacity building as a leadership stance underscores how applied research for sustainable change is an approach to transformational educational leadership practices that cultivates change from within educational organizations.

We've used the term *resource-oriented capacity building* to make clear that a leader should focus on the resources, insights, and knowledge that colleagues and staff bring to research teams rather than view what these individuals lack as a deficiency of some sort. In building your team's capacity, you must pay attention to all the capacity that already exists on your team. You need to resist deficit thinking, which, among other things, may suggest to staff that you think they lack some capacity and that this deficit might somehow hurt their job standing.[5] Thus, you must clearly demonstrate your respect for your staff's *wisdom of practice*.[6] Framing all this as integrated professional development can help offset potential concerns from team members. This resource-oriented capacity building begins with you, the leader. In the current education environment, and for many decades earlier, we have seen a decline in the professionalization of teachers and other educators. This de-professionalization and disrespect for educators must be disrupted at every turn, especially in today's high-stakes, test-driven environment.[7]

POWER DYNAMICS

Because power is inherent in everyday life, power dynamics come into play in collaborative research. As the leader of your school, organization, or district, you will want to consider how your involvement as the leader affects the people on the research team and others involved in the research. We continue to address issues of power throughout the book, but stress here that in collaborative research, power differentials and implicit hierarchies on research teams can impede open collaboration. As the leader, you need to expressly position yourself as a learner so that others on the team can feel that their contributions are important and taken seriously. Furthermore, as you seek to build the capacity of your research team and staff and foster shared accountability, you can model what reciprocal accountability looks like and create spaces for dialogue and reflection in team meetings.

From a research perspective, the way that data are collected is directly related to the quality of the data and findings. Since data become the foundation of arguments for particular actions, you need to understand the role of power in research teams and with research participants. Power dynamics can be based on social identities (i.e., intersections of gender, race, social class, and so on), social power, years of experience. You also need to recognize power as someone with an evaluator and how power manifests itself in seemingly mundane conversations and other situations.

A first step in addressing power dynamics is to openly acknowledge them instead of pretending they are not there. For example, Eleanor (see chapter 1) navigated power differentials as a superintendent by having a direct discussion with her principals. To begin this discussion, she told them, "I am your boss, and I understand that this dynamic will not go away. However, it is something that I am very mindful of, and I encourage you to conduct this kind of collaborative research with your own staff. In this shared effort, we are all learners working to solve a problem." Although a leader's power does not go away, Eleanor worked to cultivate shared accountability with her principals and position herself as a learner open to taking risks.

Another consideration for leaders is how individuals counter power. If there are no direct ways for individuals' concerns to be heard, people will inevitably challenge authority through indirect means. This is an important lesson for leaders of all kinds. Leaders need to ask themselves how they are creating spaces for voices to be heard and acknowledged. Applied research can be used to engage those who feel unheard, unseen, or otherwise marginalized. But it can only be used for good if the tools of this research are themselves examined critically. You have to look at the representation (e.g., social identity groups, stakeholder groups, affinity groups, community members) of the individuals on your team as well as the invited study participants. You also need to understand what the research priorities are and why they formed. Finally, you should examine how meetings can be structured so that all the members feel they have had a fair chance to be heard and feel safe enough to risk sharing things that may be unpopular or commonly misunderstood or that may highlight their feelings or vulnerabilities.

BRAVE SPACES

When a group is discussing issues that some people might find challenging or in which people may have strongly held beliefs, a common solution has been to create safe spaces for conversation.[8] The term *safe space* has come to mean a place where everyone feels comfortable to speak freely and to share any experiences, feelings, concerns, and so on.[9] However, the concept of safe spaces can be a setup for many individuals and groups because *safe* means different things to different people, and so what feels safe to one person might feel hostile, overly polite, inauthentic, marginalizing, or negligent to another.

In contrast to safe spaces, brave spaces require more bravery in your leadership and more ongoing support so that people can discuss issues at the heart of education, going a layer deeper than typical discussions in schools.[10] Table 4.1 summarizes the distinctions between the two kinds of spaces so that you can decide how to incorporate these ideas in your applied research team meetings.

In light of our decades-long work in schools and classrooms, we believe that even the act of introducing the concept of a brave space marks the beginning of a group's deciding how it wants to work together. When educators are personally uncomfortable having discussions about equity, identity, and so on, they are often ill-equipped to engage with their students, colleagues, and the rest of the school community about these topics.[11] Thus, it is important for educational leaders to promote having these kinds of discussions in schools and districts.

Discussing the difference between safe spaces and brave spaces has been powerful in our work with applied research teams in schools and districts. Brave spaces become especially important during applied research team meetings, because personal lenses and biases influence all aspects of the research, including the research questions and how the researchers collect and analyze

TABLE 4.1 Differences between safe and brave spaces

SAFE SPACES	BRAVE SPACES
▪ Prioritize politeness	▪ Prioritize honesty and authenticity
▪ Value comfort when discussing difficult issues	▪ Acknowledge discomfort as inevitable in discussions of difficult issues
▪ Can lead to defensiveness and deflection	▪ Value risk taking, vulnerability, and being challenged
▪ Narrowly define safety, usually stemming from a dominant perspective	▪ Contend that safety means different things to different people and groups
▪ Tend not to prepare participants for difficult conversations	▪ Prepare groups for difficult conversations

Source: Brian Arao and Kristi Clemens, "From Safe Spaces to Brave Spaces: A New Way to Frame Dialogue Around Diversity and Social Justice," in *The Art of Effective Facilitation: Reflections from Social Justice Educators*, ed. Lisa M. Landreman (Sterling, VA: Stylus Publishing, 2013), 135–150.

data. To make sure the applied research is ethical, the team needs a space to have difficult conversations.

For example, when we work with applied research teams on issues of implicit bias in teaching, we often see examples of societal tropes that people fall into. For instance, there's the well-meaning white woman who tries to be racially aware but who says things that are offensive or who is overly emotional about her own white pain and guilt at society's inequity. Or there's the woman of color who is interpreted negatively as an "angry black woman" or "hostile Latinx woman" before she even gets one full sentence out. Or a team has a white man who tries to eschew his racial and gender privilege by talking about his own family's meritocracy story. But although countless people do not fall into these stereotypical buckets, you and your team should recognize that these cultural and racial identity tropes exist. Understanding the crucial concepts of microaggressions (see chapter 2) and implicit bias (chapter 7) can be a helpful place to start. We discuss strategies for how to cocreate brave spaces with your staff and colleagues in the final section of this chapter.

SIZE AND MAKEUP OF APPLIED RESEARCH TEAMS

Understanding how groups operate is a central skill in leading or even being a part of any team. Educational stakeholders on applied research teams are likely to have different priorities, and for the team to be successful, its members should share a clear, common goal. This is often easier said than done. A majority of teams working in organizations are unclear about their purpose, goals, and rationale.[12] Furthermore, other commonsense ideas about what makes a team successful, including considerations of size, goals, skills, approach, and accountability, are often not put into practice.[13]

There are no uniform answers to these considerations. For example, the size of a team will often vary, but as common sense would dictate, the larger the team, the harder it is to agree on goals and vision. We recommend that applied research teams are composed of no more than ten people. Of course, exceptions can be made, but once a team is larger than ten, additional challenges (e.g., scheduling, attendance inconsistencies, and the ability to hide in a large group) often arise.

Who should be on your research team? The answer depends on many factors, including organizational culture and dynamics, human resources and schedules, and the focus of the research. If your research examines issues of racial unease between students, you would want to have on your team individuals with different perspectives on and experiences with race, racial identity, racial literacy, and racial unease. Table 4.2 presents questions to help guide you as you form a research team.

TABLE 4.2 Considerations for forming a research team

Topical considerations	
• What problem or other issue are we studying? • Why are we studying this issue here and now? • In a similar vein, what different perspectives should we try to include on our team?	• What individuals at the school, in the community, or from other organizations should potentially be on the research team? What groups and perspectives do they represent?
Organizational factors	
• What institutional or community resistance might there be to this topic or to research in general? • Who are the influential voices in this organization? What kinds of influence do they have?	• Should some of these individuals be on the team? Why or why not? • What are the potential consequences or other considerations for including some people and not others on the team?
Basic considerations: Size and time	
• What is an ideal size for the team? • Is there a dedicated time that all these individuals can meet? When and for how long?	• If not, how and when will the team meet? Does this scheduling challenge perhaps mean that we need to change who is on the team so that they can all be present together?
Skills	
• What skills should members of the team have? For example, is there a person familiar with research approaches? Do we know of anyone skilled in facilitation, organizational development, dissemination, and other practices? Are there people who have great emotional intelligence and who can help us construct an engaging and productive research environment by helping to foster thoughtful team dynamics and effective teamwork?	• How will the rest of the team members acquire the appropriate skills to conduct this research? • Can there be focused professional and skills development at the outset? How will this work?

LEADING APPLIED RESEARCH TEAMS

Of course, one of the first steps in leading an applied research team is to make sure everyone on the team clearly understands the group's goals, roles, and norms.[14] Let's look at each of these elements in turn.

Team Goals

As discussed in chapter 3, agreeing on clear, shared goals can be a challenge for applied research teams. The members have many perspectives, backgrounds, and experiences and may disagree on why the research is important. Thus, developing collective goals for the team is crucial to ensuring that the team is aligned in its work. To develop these goals, team members may want to learn about each other's visions and beliefs and then consider together what unifies their collective work. This recommendation does not necessarily mean that individuals change their personal goals, but it does mean that the team agrees on what it is trying to accomplish. Furthermore, throughout the process of determining shared goals, team members gain a broader understanding of the others' perspectives. Once the collaborative goals and visions are developed, team members should commit to revisit and check in on the progress toward their team's goals.[15]

Team Roles

The roles of team members refer to the formal and informal aspects of how a team is run. When they have clear roles, the team members are aware of their responsibilities. Many of you have probably been on a team in which no one knows who is responsible for what. A common consequence is that one or two individuals end up doing the work because of fear that it will not get done otherwise. This approach is antithetical to our collaborative research stance, in which we assert that the collaborative power of applied research teams is what generates research and action that can be sustainable. Thus, specific roles for each team member should be clearly delineated.

Many roles may evolve once a research design has been developed (see chapter 3). However, other roles related to running the team and team meetings can be developed before you develop a research plan. For example, the team can decide who will lead the team meetings and who will develop the agenda. It could also decide if these roles will rotate. Will the same person always be responsible for these tasks, or will the tasks rotate between different members? Another important role is the check-in leader. All members of the team should ideally be committed to checking in and ensuring that everyone agrees with the goals, roles, and norms. However, assigning this role to one person can help ensure that this commitment remains someone's priority. The role also gives leadership to an individual who can think about creative ways to monitor the functioning of the team.

Team Norms

Norms exist on teams, whether these guidelines are established or not. When they are not collaboratively discussed or agreed on, problematic norms may develop to fill the void. For example, if there is no shared understanding of how to address conflict on teams, individuals may deal with disagreement in unproductive ways. Without a norm for how group discussions are led, the most outspoken team members may tend to dominate conversations. Another example relates to the use of computers or smart devices during meetings. It is quite common for individuals to have laptops or phones out during meetings even though these tools can be distracting. Regardless of your belief about these and other issues, your team needs to address them proactively for the productivity and collegiality of the team, especially when conflicts or other challenges arise.

The best way to proactively address challenges to group dynamics is to regularly check in with team members to see if they still commit to the team goals, roles, and norms and to openly discuss any changes that need to be made in how the group operates.[16] These processes of discussion and negotiation should be visible and shared within the group. Although you and others may sometimes check in with one another outside group time, being judicious and intentional about your communication is important. We urge the leaders we work with to encourage clear communication so as to avoid "toxic triangulation," in which

TABLE 4.3   Considerations for group norms

- How long and how often will the meetings be?
- What structure will we follow for the meetings?
- Will certain processes be in place for different stages of the meetings (e.g., raising issues in a set order and prioritizing topics)?
- What is expected of team members during meetings?
- What work should happen between meetings? How will the work be shared? How do people ask for help and share questions as they do their tasks?
- How will we distribute the responsibility of note-taking during meetings? Will this duty rotate?
- How should team members speak during the meeting (e.g., using a talking stick, raising hands, jumping in)?
- How can the group elicit a range of perspectives?
- How will we make decisions (e.g., consensus, majority vote)?
- What is considered unacceptable behavior in meetings? Why?
- How might social identities factor into different behaviors and interpretations of group dynamics?
- How will we view and address conflict?
- What other principles guide our group work?

one member of the group receives a message indirectly from another member, and the roundabout messaging leads to confusion and mistrust.[17] Thus, as the leader, you should clearly establish—and follow—guidelines on how feedback and other communication will be delivered. Table 4.3 suggests topics that teams can collaboratively discuss to develop productive team norms.

STORIES FROM THE FIELD

Facilitating Research Team Dynamics

Sarah is the director of curriculum and instruction for two schools in the Excellence Charter High Schools in a southwestern US suburb. Over the past year, she has watched the local public high schools gradually expand their dual-credit course offerings, so that students can earn high school and college credit for their academic work and thus get a head start on their college degrees. Students and parents in the Excellence community have noticed this trend, too, and have started to express concerns that the charter schools offer no comparable dual-credit options. With these concerns in mind, Sarah decided to assemble a team to conduct applied research on the possibility of building a dual-credit program for the Excellence charter school network.

Sarah knew that to make sustainable changes, she had to include a range of perspectives on the issue. First, she reached out to the lead science and math coordinator and the lead literacy coordinator for the Excellence network. These individuals' perspectives would be important because of their insight about the current course syllabi and graduation requirements. Sarah also recruited the principal and director of college counseling from each school to be on the research team as well as one school's registrar, who could speak to the impact of dual-credit courses on student records and front-office processes. Sarah and the other staff members held an initial meeting to discuss various opinions about the topic, and they all decided that the next step would be to host a town hall meeting for students and parents to share their opinions about dual-credit programs. Members of the school staff also attended the event and were instructed to take careful notes about students' and parents' opinions. Sarah approached one student and parent who were especially passionate about the issue and asked them to join the team. The applied research team now consisted of ten members, including Sarah.

Now that Sarah assembled the applied research team, she needed to work on balancing competing priorities. For example, the curricular coordinators were worried about how their teachers would react to new grading policies. One principal was concerned that some of the colleges that students were applying to would not accept these credits. The parent on the team wondered if the children attending Excellence schools were receiving the same advantages that the children attending the district schools were enjoying.

Sarah told the team members that through this applied research, they would gain the much-needed information to guide their decisions. She also realized that she needed to spend some time developing group rapport and trust and establishing clear goals, roles, and norms for their shared work. Thus,

Sarah began starting the meetings with quick icebreakers, which she facilitated by asking various people in the group to suggest warm-up group-building activities that people would find meaningful and inspiring (rather than Pollyanna and annoying, as is often the case with these kinds of things).

The group was progressing well, and after focused group conversations about goals, roles, and norms, Sarah began to realize that she should not lead every meeting. The team decided to develop a schedule in which other team members could sign up to lead meetings. This rotation of the meeting leaders helped increase the sense of shared accountability, as everyone on the team was responsible for moving the goals forward.

Sarah and the team devoted several meetings to creating clear norms for how conflict would be handled. One norm was to reserve time in every meeting for honest disagreement. However, because of different power dynamics, it was clear that not everyone would necessarily feel comfortable speaking up. Thus, the team fashioned a box in which individuals would deposit comments at the end of a meeting. These comments tended to include topics for the team to discuss at the next meeting, but to keep the notes completely anonymous, everyone would add a comment to the box as one of the closing rituals. Sarah would read all the comments and bring issues to the table for the team to discuss at its next meeting.

This example highlights how Sarah effectively led a team of multiple stakeholders and established shared goals, roles, and norms. Doing this took multiple team meetings, but the members solely focused on team dynamics during three meetings. At the other meetings, they also worked on other aspects of the research process.

PRACTICES TO START

As the example highlights, developing trust through the establishment of clear goals, roles, and norms is central to leading an effective team. In the following practices, we discuss ways for teams to develop trust and reflexivity.

PRACTICE 10: *Assessing Biases and Blind Spots*

As a leader, you need to model a reflexive approach to research. One part of this approach involves acknowledging biases and blind spots. It can be difficult to see your own blind spots, and thus engaging in these practices both individually and collectively can be beneficial to everyone and can create trust among research team members.

Structure these reflections by encouraging questions about your values, potential biases, and potential blind spots, and have your team members do the same. Examples of questions include the following:

- What am I passionate about? What guides this passion?
- What are my educational priorities? Why these and not others?
- How does this passion or priority play out in my practice as an educator?
- How might this passion or priority lead to biases? Which biases?
- What could be the result of these biases?
- How might this passion or priority lead to blind spots in my practice as an educator? What are possible implications of these blind spots?
- What prejudices do I have about specific social identity groups? Professional groups? Social classes? What evidence do I have that challenges these prejudices?
- How could the school, district, or other organization be a more inclusive and resonant place for all people?
- Who is often left out when I think of the student body? The faculty? Why?
- What are my feelings about youth culture today? About the role of technology in students' lives? About youth values and beliefs?
- Am I biased toward students, teachers, or parents with various mental health issues or learning differences? If so, in what ways?
- What frustrates me or makes me anxious about professional discussions about equity? Why?
- Am I aware of how my social identity (i.e., the intersections of race, gender, culture, religion, and other social factors) shapes my

thinking? How does it shape how others perceive me? What about how I perceive them?

A suggested process would first involve time for personal reflection of these questions and then small-group discussion about how biases might function as blind spots both in educational settings as well as in research. Resource E reproduces these questions in tabular format for you to use and share with your team.

PRACTICE 11: *Introducing and Cocreating Brave Spaces*

As discussed earlier in this chapter, creating brave spaces can be an important way to engage people in constructive critique. For this reason, we offer several ideas for creating with your research team some guidelines for brave spaces.

We recommend that you (or another team member) introduce the term *brave space* with the team. You might ask the members why they think you are using that term (rather than the more familiar term *safe space*) and then discuss why you have chosen the term. After this initial discussion, the team members could develop a shared definition of what a brave space would be for them and then could discuss how to create such a space over the duration of the group's shared work. Throughout this process, we recommend that you (or the person leading these sessions) model openness to the other participants' ideas and a desire to involve everyone in the discussion. One way to do this is to affirm people's input, engaging with them even if they are struggling with the concept of brave spaces or with other seemingly basic concepts. It is important to remember and remind others that people come from various places and vantage points and have unique ways of seeing the world. At a subsequent meeting, you might consider returning to the concept of braves spaces and selecting an article to read together that builds on Arao and Clemens's brave space framework.

After agreeing on what brave spaces are, you and your team might take time to collectively set norms for group discussions of topics that may be considered controversial or otherwise difficult. Ideally, the team works on these norms together and then makes a written summary of them easily available to everyone. The process that you use for setting team norms will depend on a variety of factors, including how much time is available for a given discussion. Whichever procedure you choose, treat the activity as a valuable part of the learning process, not only as a precursor to it or something to get through quickly. Group norms are influenced by many factors, including the team membership, people's familiarity with each other, and how people engage with each other. Drawing on Brian Arao and Kristi Clemens's research, we present examples of norms for brave teams:

- Handle controversy with civility.
- Own your intentions and your impact.
- Engage in active reflexivity.
- Codefine respect.
- Clarify individual and system beliefs.[18]

As you and the team develop and review the norms for brave spaces, you can invite participants to think critically about how the norms might help or hinder authentic and productive discussion.

Another way to engage team members in the concept of brave spaces is to develop a group statement related to cultivating brave spaces. For example, the following statement is one that we share with leaders:

> It is crucial that we all take responsibility for creating a community in which open and respectful dialogue can occur. We encourage risk-taking in ourselves and others and support respectfully and actively challenging each other on important issues, with the goal of promoting learning for all. We collectively work to create a space where we can discuss our differing perspectives without being judged. For this to happen, we recognize that we are all growing and learning together and understand that everyone holds dear certain points of view and has unique perspectives about the world.

As with all practices in this book, we recommend adapting and refining them to make them as relevant and useful as possible to your circumstances.

CHAPTER SUMMARY

This chapter presents our approach to collaborative research through participation in applied research teams. We detailed three attitudes for you and your team members to consider when enacting collaborative research: (1) a willingness to seek out and learn from multiple perspectives, (2) a commitment to shared learning and knowledge through research, and (3) an openness to change. This chapter discussed important considerations for forming an applied research team, whose composition may vary depending on the topic, organizational culture, time constraints, and individual skills. Furthermore, we examined how collaboratively defining the goals, roles, and norms of a team is central to leading an effective applied research team, and we presented important considerations for codeveloping group norms. We also shared an example of how Sarah, a director of curriculum and instruction at a charter school network, facilitated and successfully led an applied research ream. Finally, the chapter detailed practices for building trust and fostering reflexivity among team members, discussing biases and blind spots, and creating brave spaces for discussing difficult topics.

FIVE

Collecting Useful and Actionable Data

THIS CHAPTER BUILDS on the applied research design processes presented in chapter 3 and discusses the central role of research questions in data collection. We describe the primary data collection strategies and methods and how they directly align with a study's research question. Among the methods we examine are interviews, focus groups, fieldnotes, preexisting data, surveys, photovoice, and mapping. We also discuss how to develop the kinds of research instruments you will use to collect data. And we continue discussing the example of Charles and his applied research team studying literacy instruction (see chapter 3). This time, we demonstrate how the team developed instruments and collected data to answer their research questions.

In this chapter, we show how to collect useful and actionable data so that the findings are reliable enough to inform potential changes and other decisions. You will learn methods for promoting research validity during data collection. These methods include conducting participant validation, incorporating multiple perspectives and data sources, using reflexive strategies, and collaboratively engaging with members of your research team. To animate what this looks like in practice, we present examples of how a superintendent used these validity processes during an applied research study in her district. The chapter concludes with specific practices to help your applied research team begin to collect useful and valid data.

We consider the following questions throughout this chapter:

- What is the role of research questions in applied research?
- How do you align data collection methods with your research questions?
- What are the primary data collection methods you will use?
- What should you consider when developing research instruments for interviews, focus groups, and observations?
- How do you decide the relevance of existing data sources?
- What are the key issues affecting the validity of your applied research, and how do you address them?

THE CENTRALITY OF RESEARCH QUESTIONS

Research questions are at the center of decisions about what data to collect. For example, research questions guide the methods you use to collect your data (e.g., interviews, focus groups, surveys); the sampling decisions about where and from whom you will collect your data (i.e., the research setting and the participants involved); and the **research instruments**, or the tools you use to collect your data. These tools include the questions you will ask during an interview or focus group or what you will look for in an observation.

As noted earlier, applied research teams often refine their questions during a study. However, these changes tend to be related to how a question is worded and what it seeks to learn. Changes to the research topic and focus, in contrast, might result in a new study. Thus, as you and your team consider your methods, we strongly recommend that you consider how they align with your research questions. Table 5.1 suggests questions that you and your team can ask as you decide on methods, participants, and instruments; we revisit these questions at the end of the chapter. Carefully considering these questions and

TABLE 5.1 Aligning decisions about methods, sampling, and instruments to research questions

RESEARCH QUESTIONS	METHODS	SAMPLING	INSTRUMENTS
• What are the guiding research questions (RQs)? • Do these RQs capture what you want to learn more about? Why or why not? • Do you need to make any changes to the RQs? • If so, what changes?	• What methods will you use to get the necessary data to answer the RQs? • What is your rationale for using these methods?	• Where and from whom will you collect data? • What participants will be involved in the study? Why? • How will you recruit participants? • What preexisting data are needed to answer the RQs? Why?	• What instruments do you need to develop? • How will you design instruments to answer the RQs? • What kind of information will these instruments help you collect? • Who can help you know if the instruments are properly customized for various stakeholder groups?

the rationale for your choices helps to ensure that your methods, participant sampling, and instruments are clearly connected to your research questions.

DATA COLLECTION STRATEGIES AND METHODS

There are many ways to collect data for applied research projects. These methods, which we introduced in chapter 3, include interviews, focus groups, fieldnotes, surveys, preexisting data, photovoice, and mapping. You select your methods in light of your guiding research questions as well as time, logistics, and resources. In this section, we discuss important considerations for each possible data collection method. Figure 5.1 presents an overview of these data collection methods.

Interviews

Considered the hallmark of qualitative research, interviews provide researchers with focused insight about an individual's contextualized experience. The

FIGURE 5.1 Data collection methods in applied research

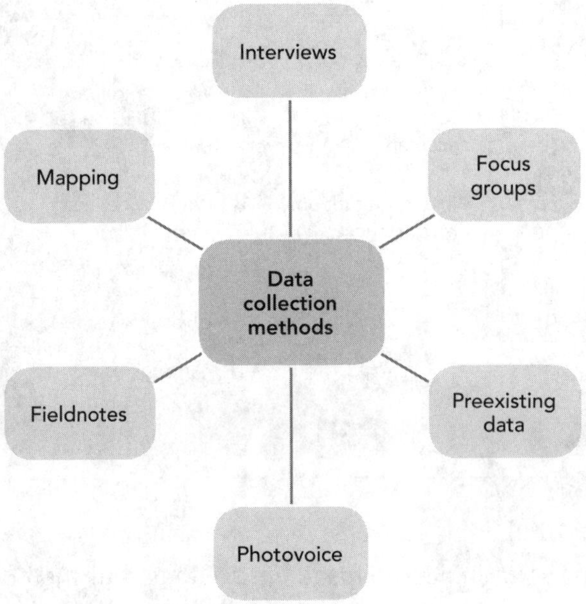

- Interviews
- Focus groups
- Preexisting data
- Photovoice
- Fieldnotes
- Mapping

(Center: Data collection methods)

use of interviews conducted across a group of individuals allows your team to develop contextualized descriptions of experiences, understand and compare multiple perspectives, and encourage a broad appreciation of all the elements that come into play for the issue in question.[1]

In applied research studies, you will largely conduct *semistructured interviews*, that is, interviews for which you develop a list of the questions you plan to ask participants. However, you can and probably will deviate from this list to ask follow-up questions. You might also ask the questions in a different-from-planned order. We recommend that interviewers remain flexible during the interview. For example, if an interviewee answers a future question in responding to a different question, you should either skip the future question or ask for clarifying information when you get to the later question.

If you are interviewing different groups of participants, you will need different instruments for each group, even if the questions are similarly worded. For example, if you are interviewing students and teachers, the interview instrument for students would be different from, although still somewhat similar, to the one for teachers. For adult interviews, the instrument should have approximately ten questions if it is a forty-five-minute interview. Of course, the number of questions depends on the type and content of questions and on how much time you have. However, this guideline allows time for follow-up questions (e.g., asking for examples and clarification), which help you to collect useful and valid data. For interviews with students, you can include more questions on your instrument and should plan for shorter interviews since youth's responses—and, therefore, interviews—tend to be briefer.

The type of questions you ask participants depends on your research questions. In general, as a part of the interview, you ask questions that help you explore each person's experiences, behaviors, opinions, and emotions. Besides obtaining personal background information that is relevant to the research, you also ask about the individual's knowledge about an event, a situation, or an issue.[2]

When conducting an interview, you should begin by informing the participants about the process. Be sure to inform them that they do not have to answer a question if they do not feel comfortable. Other things to share with them include how long the interview will last, how their information will be used and protected, who will have access to the data, and whom they should contact if they have questions after the interview. Then you obtain written or verbal consent (depending on the sensitive nature of the study as well as the formal procedures required for your educational organization) before beginning the interview. In addition, if you want to audio-record the interview using a digital recorder, you need to request permission to do so. We discussed informed consent and assent processes further in chapter 3.

We highly recommend audio-recording interviews, focus groups, observations, and the like, when possible because recording people's actual words makes the analysis of the data considerably more reliable. If you cannot audio-record the interview, ideally an additional team member can attend the interview so that one person can take notes while the other engages with the interview participant. If that is not an option, you will need to take notes during the interview as unobtrusively as possible and then, immediately after the interview, fill in and add to your notes to capture as much of what was said as possible. In table 5.2, we have compiled helpful strategies for developing interview and focus group instruments.

You should always rehearse by asking a colleague the questions on your interview instrument so that you become familiar with them and do not feel compelled to stare at your list of questions during the interview. By being familiar with your questions, you can more fully engage with the participants and listen attentively during the actual interview. Research teams we have advised report appreciating our recommendation that team members practice interviewing each other. They found that the practice helped them refine any awkwardly worded or unclear questions on the instrument. Rehearsing also gave them a better understanding of what it feels like to be interviewed. Both these benefits helped them feel better prepared and more engaged in the interviews and focus groups that they conducted.

TABLE 5.2 Tips for developing interview and focus group instruments

- Many interviewers include too many questions. As a rule of thumb, it's difficult to conduct a forty-five- to sixty-minute interview with more than ten predetermined questions.
- Focus group instruments should have approximately five predetermined questions.
- Begin the interview or focus group with a clear description of the process and timing.
- Have as many open-ended questions (i.e., questions requiring more than a yes or no answer) as possible.
- Ask for specific examples of processes, events, and experiences, and ask people to explain why these cases illustrate a specific feeling or phenomenon.
- Avoid leading questions, which set up a forced answer.
- Make questions as simple and direct as possible; do not use jargon or other confusing terms.
- Think about the flow of questions, and make sure they are asked in a logical order.
- For your last question, ask the participants if they would like to add anything else to the interview or focus group. Allow time for them to consider and respond.

STORIES FROM THE FIELD

Developing an Interview Instrument

Jennifer, an assistant head of school at Middleberry Independent School, became concerned about the school's ninth-grade students' scores on a nationally normed survey. The students reported much higher levels of stress than did the other grades at the school and ninth-grade students at other independent schools. Jennifer formed an applied research team to learn more about ninth-grade students and their experiences. The goal was a better understanding of why these students were reporting such high levels of stress and how the school could better support the children. The applied research team developed the following research questions:

- What are the experiences of ninth-grade students at Middleberry?
- What are these students' primary stressors and other challenges?
- How can the school better support these students?

The team decided to conduct interviews with teachers and students, send an open-ended survey to all ninth-grade students, and observe students in several locations. The team also decided to review preexisting data, including data the school already had about the amount of time students spent on their school laptops. Jennifer and the applied research team began by interviewing teachers to gain a better sense of the questions they would ask students in interviews and in the survey. In addition, the team believed that the interviews with teachers would help the researchers determine what they would focus on during observations.

Resource F reproduces the team's first draft of the interview instrument, including the questions that the team planned to ask teachers, advisers, and counselors. This is an example of a set of interview questions that have been developed in accordance with the goals of the study and the guiding research questions. You will notice that some aspects are left blank and are to be filled in during the interview. In other parts of the instrument, a script is provided to help guide the interviewer. Finally, at the very end of the instrument, there is also a place for the interviewer to add additional notes or ideas.

Focus Groups

Focus groups are sometimes referred to as group interviews. Whatever their name, they present a unique opportunity for a team to see how a group of people think about, collectively respond to, and experience an issue. The goal of focus groups in applied research is to have the participants—no more than six or seven, so that everyone has a chance to participate—respond to each other as they discuss a topic. As one person mentions a topic or responds to a question, other participants respond by sharing their perspectives in ways that might not have been included without the combined insight of the other participants. As a researcher conducting a focus group, you act more as a facilitator than an interviewer. Your role is to keep the dialogue going, help people respond to each other, refocus the group if it gets off-topic, and make sure that everyone has sufficient time to share their perspectives and to present questions to the group.

There are different ways to arrange the participants in focus groups, and the rationale for each grouping depends on your research questions. While focus groups with colleagues and employees have the benefits of generating contextualized data, they may present additional challenges. For example, the participants may hesitate to discuss certain topics, given that coworkers are present. You cannot guarantee **confidentiality** in a focus group, because you, as the researcher, cannot ensure that other individuals in the focus group will not share what is discussed. We always begin focus groups in the same way that we begin interviews: we ask the members to keep what is shared within the group confidential and respect each other's privacy. You need to remind the participants that there is always some risk in participation, given that confidentiality cannot be guaranteed, and that, because of these risks, their discretion is vital to ensuring comfort both during and after the focus group.

Like interviews, focus groups typically have a semistructured approach. That is, you will probably have an instrument comprising a list of questions to guide the conversation. Focus groups typically have fewer questions than do individual interviews. Thus, for a focus group composed of six adults and lasting forty-five minutes, you should have approximately five questions in addition to an opener, in which the individuals introduce themselves if they do not know each other. Again, the number of questions depends greatly on the content and type of questions as well as how talkative the members of a focus group are. If you have many questions on your instrument, make sure that you first ask your high-priority questions, including any follow-up prompts that you wish to ask, and that you hear from everyone before you move on to other questions.

Focus groups, like interviews, are ideally audio-recorded (with participants' permission). Logistically, it can also be helpful to have two team members conduct a focus group so that one person can take notes, as developing transcripts from focus groups can be more challenging. With two people acting as facilitators, one person can focus on the flow of conversation while the other carefully records the data. Finally, have members of your research team help you and other members practice conducting a focus group. This rehearsal helps you and your team develop research skills and refine your focus groups questions (see table 5.2 for more tips).

Taking Notes During Interviews and Focus Groups

In school-based research, your notes from interviews and focus groups form reliable data that you can use to make sense of what people actually said. As mentioned above, audio-recording all interviews will give you the option of returning to the recording should any confusion arise (or should people later forget what was said). Furthermore, whenever possible, you should conduct interviews and focus groups in pairs so that one person can take notes as the other facilitates. Working in pairs means that the two of you can debrief afterward, thereby enhancing, and sometimes challenging, your team's interpretations of what the participants said in the interviews or focus groups and how this acquired information applies to the research questions and goals. To record what happened in a way that will be valid and useful to your future analysis, write your notes directly on the instrument (the paper with the interview questions and prompts) during the interview or focus group and then, as soon as possible, turn these observations into more detailed notes after each interview or focus group. Refer back to the audio-recordings when needed, especially if you wish to use verbatim quotes in reports or otherwise need the exact words of the participants' statements.

Fieldnotes

You can use observational data, which are documented in fieldnotes, many ways in applied research. The method of observing and capturing your observations in written fieldnotes stems from the anthropological method of *participant observation*. In this method, an individual is immersed in a setting and constantly observes and takes fieldnotes as a way to understand the contextual meanings embedded in people's daily lives. Participant observation is a more in-depth observational method and can sometimes be used in applied research studies, depending on the research questions. For example, if you as a leader are taking fieldnotes about an aspect of your own daily practice, you would be using a form of participant observation: you are immersed in the setting and are systematically observing and taking fieldnotes. As you can see, then, there are multiple ways to use observational data, including observing your own and others' activities. However, both methods require the systematic recording of fieldnotes.

The *systematic* part of this definition is important. For observational data to be rigorous, it must be systematically captured in fieldnotes. A first step in writing fieldnotes often includes writing brief notes, or *jottings*, during an observation. After jotting down the in-the-moment observations, the researcher turns these jottings into detailed fieldnotes. You need to write your fieldnotes as soon as you can after the actual observation, to avoid potentially forgetting what happened and not understanding your jottings. While your jottings can be handwritten, we recommend fleshing out your fieldnotes on a computer. Some people prefer handwriting their jottings, and others prefer typing them. Members of your team can decide on their preference for jotting notes. You may want to use a method that is the least obtrusive in a setting.

In addition to participant observation, fieldnote data are often collected to observe specific events or settings. For example, Charles, the assistant principal discussed in chapter 3, and his team each observed two teachers during a literacy lesson. For these types of specific observations, team members often use a printed observational instrument that guides what they are looking for. Researchers may also jot their notes directly on this guide while they observe. After the observation, team members type up their fieldnotes or completely fill in the observational guide.

Observation is a main part of applied research projects. As soon as you begin engaging in research in your institution, you are taking in new kinds of data. Once you train yourself to observe carefully, you will be amazed at the things going on right in front of you that you did not previously notice. During an observation, there are many aspects to pay attention to. In general, your observational focus depends on the research questions and goals of the observation. In resource G, we suggest potential aspects to note when you are observing a classroom or another school-based setting. Not all these aspects will be relevant to the setting or the research focus, but this list can get you started on what to note.

As is the case with all data collection methods, the ability of fieldnotes to produce data that help answer your research questions depends on your research goals. For example, when Charles and his team wanted to understand the school's approach to literacy, they needed to find out how different teachers approached teaching literacy. Thus, observational data was an important part of the team's research design. Charles's team used an open-ended observational instrument similar to the one found in resource H.

When collecting observational data, you, as the educational leader and head learner, need to communicate that these observations are not evaluative. Instead, the goal is to learn. Furthermore, you should separate as much as possible your interpretations from your descriptions in your jottings and fieldnotes. Try to refrain from giving your opinion or judgment about what is happening. For example, if you are observing a teacher whom you find personally annoying, this opinion should be omitted from your notes unless the annoying trait somehow affects an observation connected to the research questions. Keeping interpretation out of your observations is challenging, as the way people describe something is influenced by their interpretations. Although this interpretation cannot be eliminated, it is important to be as systematically neutral as possible. In the next two paragraphs, we discuss some ways to productively approach observations and fieldnotes.

When you enter a building or meeting, what do you notice? What stands out? To look with new eyes, try to walk in as if you were coming into the space for the first time. Try to be aware of any biases that you might be bringing with you. You might consider jotting these down on paper to try to consciously put them aside. The primary task of an observer is to notice and describe rather than judge or evaluate. For example, in a staff meeting, you observe what's going on. A judgmental observation might read as follows: "Every time Joe speaks, the principal treats him like an idiot." A descriptive frame would instead be more akin to the following: "Every time Joe speaks, the principal starts tapping his fingers on the table, looks around the room, rolls his eyes, raises his eyebrows, and, nine times out of ten, says, 'That's fine' to Joe."

It takes practice to describe the behaviors you see instead of your judgment or analyses. We also recommend using all your senses—not just what you see—to make observations around you (e.g., school bells ringing, students' laughter, and outdoor smells wafting in from the windows). When using observation as a primary method, you will want to observe in a way that gives you representative data about the institution. For example, you can observe at the same time of day or during the same type of event over time, you can observe different locations in an organization, or you can observe different parts of an organization for one type of behavior. Other factors to pay attention to include what is said, nonverbal behavior, who does or does not speak, who interrupts whom, and if (and how) people are encouraged to speak or are silenced. In your jottings and fieldnotes, you may also want to note the location, event (e.g., meeting, conference), date, time, duration, research questions, number of people, arrangement of the setting (can be described, drawn, or photographed), time stamps, and so on.

Preexisting Data

As discussed earlier, schools are data-rich environments replete with many kinds of data that are used for a range of purposes.[3] These preexisting data sources are sometimes referred to as *archival data,* given that they live in the history of the school or district. What you and your team do with preexisting data depends on the research questions that guide what you want to learn in your study. Given that schools have so much data, you must discern which data are relevant and useful, given the topic at hand.

A first step in considering preexisting data is to decide how and if the data relate to your research questions. The multiple data sources listed in table 3.2 (chapter 3) do not become *useful* and *useable* until researchers determine that the data are relevant.[4] To make this decision, researchers must first identify and collect the data. Then they organize and review the information, including and excluding data as appropriate, and analyze them. Thus, as we describe in chapter 3, reviewing existing data sources provides important background knowledge in research design. As you begin to collect additional data, you also determine what preexisting data you will continue to review and what additional preexisting data you need to collect. Keep in mind that *more is not necessarily better*. You and your team should judiciously select and prioritize the data sources that are relevant and useful so that you are not overwhelmed by data that do not speak to the topic at hand. Later in this chapter, we discuss how Charles and his research team decided not to continue reviewing teachers' lesson plans, because these documents varied considerably and a majority contained limited information. The team's decision exemplifies how being selective about preexisting data can help ensure that the data are useful.

Surveys

Surveys comprise a set of focused questions that participants are asked. Surveys are typically conducted online but are sometimes done in person or over the phone. The survey can use open-ended, qualitative questions, for which the participants have space to write their own answers; fixed-response questions, for which the respondents select an answer from a list (sometimes a drop-down menu); or some combination of these approaches. Given the need to understand the why and how of people's responses, teams we have worked with have repeatedly told us that if they include a fixed-response question as well as a space for an explanation, the data become even more useful.

The benefits of surveys include the ability to send them to a large number of people in an efficient and cost-effective way. In addition, surveys allow participants to remain anonymous as long as identifying information is not collected. Anonymity has its trade-offs, however, since identifying information, including demographics, is a potential benefit of surveys. Finally, analyzing and compiling data can be more streamlined with surveys, and survey options like SurveyMonkey and Qualtrics can help you organize and manage your data for analysis.

Surveys do have their limitations as well. For example, the information is not as contextualized, since it is not connected to people through conversation. Therefore, you cannot ask follow-up questions. Furthermore, participants may misinterpret survey questions and respond according to what they think the question is asking.

As you develop surveys, you need to have a few people on your team go through the survey before you post it publicly so that you can refine it in light of their feedback. You want to see how long it took them to complete the survey and how they interpreted the questions (e.g., confusing wording, leading or repetitive questions). Participants are unlikely to take a survey if it takes them longer than thirty minutes to complete. If you're sending a survey to students, it should ideally take ten minutes or less for students to complete. On a similar note, you will want to consider how the survey is formatted so that it is easy to navigate.

Your survey should include an introduction that describes the survey's purpose, how the data will be used, how long the survey will take, and how individuals can get more information. The introduction should also give clear, detailed instructions for the participants. When designing surveys, you need to ensure that the questions are clearly worded so that the participants understand what you are asking. If you are going to ask the participants for demographic information, it is best to include these questions at the end of the survey. Finally, you should decide ahead of time if you want the participants to be anonymous. If you want to be able to link survey responses to various individuals, then making the survey anonymous is not a good idea.

Photovoice

Photovoice is a qualitative data collection method that you can use in multiple ways in your applied research projects. In this data collection method, participants are asked to take pictures that help them articulate their perspectives and experiences in relation to the issue being studied. The photographs could be shots of a scene, an event, an interaction, and so on. The participants are given a specific period to take their pictures, and a date is set for when everyone involved will share these photos either with members of the research team or with fellow participants and the researchers.

If you are asking adults to employ photovoice, they can use their own phones or cameras to take and then share digital images. If the participants are students, some leaders give students digital or disposable cameras to use for a specific time. Photovoice can include brief (one minute or shorter) video-recordings as well.

After individuals have taken and shared their photographs, the research team members will conduct a debrief session, either individually or as a group, with the participants. During this session, individuals will select two to five photographs and discuss why they took these pictures, what the pictures mean to them, and how the pictures relate to the research topic. After each individual presents his or her photos and narratives, the team members (or other participants if they are present) can ask questions to learn more about the person's perspectives and experiences. In this way, everyone gets a unique window into each other's individual experiences of an issue. Team members should take notes during the debrief session or audio-record it so that it can later be transcribed if desired. Careful note-taking is vital so that this information is codified as data. Memories of the experience are not data, but the carefully written and reviewed notes are. Besides being a method for collecting data, photovoice could help applied research teams and faculty members learn more about each other's perspectives.

Depending on the focus of their research, leaders have found it useful to use photovoice with a variety of stakeholder groups, including teachers, students, parents, and community members. By seeing what various people choose to photograph and then listening to their descriptions of what their photographs represent, you can obtain contextualized and nuanced data. Finally, photovoice can be adapted in many ways, depending on the participants involved and the research questions.

The guiding belief behind photovoice is that understanding what people choose to photograph is valuable. And then, as people speak and hear about the meaning of the scenes in focus, they learn a great deal about others' perceptions and experiences in a way that deepens understanding.

Mapping

You can use mapping with groups or during observations to visually represent a variety of topics, including relationships between stakeholders, power dynamics or centers of gravity in an organization, and spheres of influence in a school. The creation of these maps gives you and your team important data about culture, experiences, and perspectives, because many individuals may map a topic or setting differently. In addition, you can learn about how groups collectively map and document a place, a topic, or an event.

For example, Santiago, a superintendent of a small rural district in the Midwest, and his team of principals were studying how to improve teacher professional development in their district. The team had just begun its applied research project when Santiago, as a part of his role as superintendent, was observing a weekly professional development session for teachers at a local elementary school. He mapped the dialogue he heard during this session (figure 5.2). Santiago interpreted the dialogue, as indicated by arrows, as very one-sided, stemming primarily from the facilitator. The facilitator posed a few questions to the faculty, and they in turn directly responded to the facilitator.

FIGURE 5.2   Example of dialogue mapping

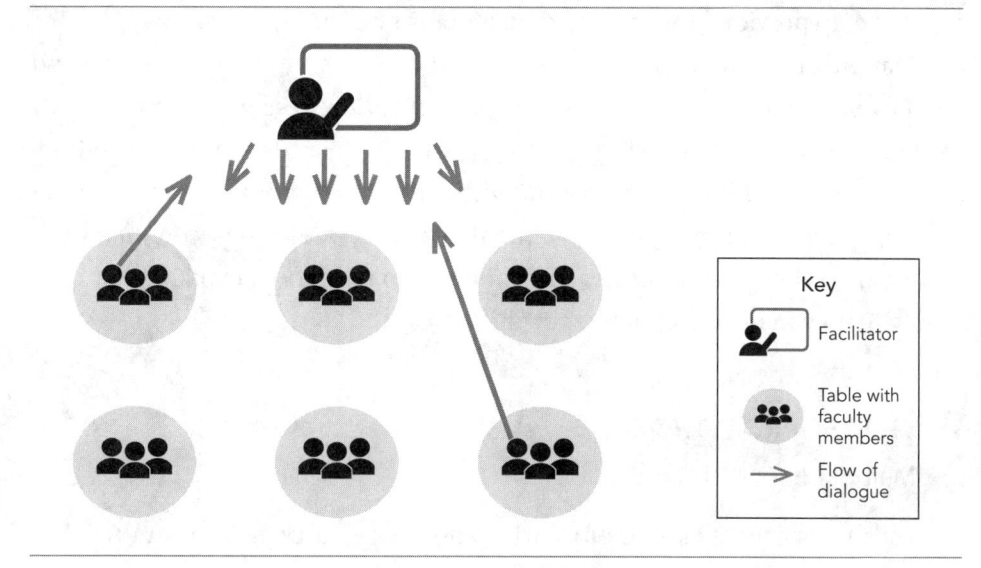

There was no exchange of information, and faculty members were not given an opportunity to discuss issues among themselves.

Santiago shared his map with the rest of the applied research team. The team decided to conduct focus groups with the faculty members to see how they experienced this professional development session and to ask them how they thought such sessions should ideally be constructed and who should lead them. The focus group started with an open-ended prompt in which the participants had about five minutes to write down what they thought an ideal professional development session would look like. Next, the participants shared their responses with the other participants. Santiago then presented his map of the faculty's most recent professional development session and asked the participants if they thought the map was an accurate representation and, if not, what he had missed and what they would map out differently and why. He also asked the participants if the mapping exercise itself could be a useful professional development session and if there are times when this type of professional development session would be more or less appropriate. The data that he and his team generated from the focus groups and other discussions regarding this map provided the team with useful insight.

Mapping is another data collection method that has many applications and can be adapted to the topic, the participants, and the research questions. For example, if you were studying an issue related to peer dynamics and school culture, you could have students, individually or as a group, create a map of the lunchroom indicating where students sit. You would then conduct a follow-up interview or focus group with students to have them explain their map and why they made the choices they did.

STORIES FROM THE FIELD
Multiple Forms of Data Collection

Let's revisit the example of Charles and his research team introduced in chapter 3. Their study of the school's approach to literacy instruction exemplifies several stages of the data collection process. Among these steps, Charles's team developed research instruments, aligned the instruments to the research questions, divided research tasks among the team members, practiced data collection methods, and refined their instruments with feedback from the entire team.

The team's guiding research questions were as follows:

- What is our school's approach to literacy instruction?
- How does (if it does) this approach vary according to grade levels and teachers?
- According to teachers, students, and the assessment data, what areas of literacy should our school prioritize?

Including Charles, there were seven members on the applied research team. As they designed their study, the team members reviewed many preexisting data sources, including standardized test scores, textbooks and curricular documents, lesson plans, excerpts from standardized tests, writing assignments and responses, and student portfolios. In addition, the team read scholarly and practitioner literature about literacy instruction to develop background knowledge. Each member also spoke informally to colleagues about their impressions of the issue to see how others understood the topic.

The research team planned to use the following methods to collect data:

- Conduct focus groups with students to have them reflect on their experiences in reading and English classes.
- Interview teachers to learn more about their approaches to teaching literacy.
- Interview each other in pairs to further document what they had learned in their group meetings as well as their own approaches to literacy instruction.
- Conduct observations and write fieldnotes to observe literacy practices in classrooms.
- Ask all teachers to respond to a qualitative prompt asking for their beliefs about literacy instruction and examples of how these beliefs are reflected in their practice.

Thus, to begin collecting all these data, the seven-member research team divided into three smaller groups. One group developed interview and focus group questions for students, teachers, and themselves. The other group continued to examine the several sources of preexisting data that the team had started to review. The third group developed an observational fieldnote instrument to be used during classroom observations; this group was also responsible for sending out the open-ended prompt to teachers.

The team developing the interview and focus group instruments needed to decide exactly who the team would be engaging with in the focus groups and interviews. Student focus groups were an important part of the research design, and the team believed that hearing from students would help the researchers better understand how students were making sense of what they were learning. Because this research is taking place at a K–8 school, the team decided to focus on eighth-grade students for a few reasons. First, some of these students had been at the school since kindergarten and would have a unique perspective in that regard. Second, the eighth graders would be able to clearly articulate their opinions and perspectives.

Resource I, a draft of the questions included in the student focus groups, demonstrates how the questions were structured to make sure they were appropriate for eighth graders. The instrument also provides an example of one way that a focus group can be facilitated. Note that the instrument includes a few more questions than may be included in a focus group with adults, because students' answers tend to be shorter than adults'. Note also that the facilitator asks the participants to spend a few minutes writing down some thoughts about the first question. This practice, which is often a good idea in all focus groups, can be done to give participants a bit of time to think before everyone begins sharing.

When Charles's research team broke up into three working groups, they set some norms for ensuring that the research progressed. Each group set an agenda that guided their time together, and the team checked in every other week as a whole group to share updates and receive feedback. During some of the whole-group meetings, the team refined interview and focus group questions and practiced conducting interviews and focus groups using a fishbowl format. In such a format, some members practice facilitating an interview and others observe the process. At another whole-group meeting, the group members responsible for reviewing the preexisting data informed the larger team that they were not going to continue reviewing teachers' lessons plans. They had decided that the lesson plans both varied considerably and were not helping them answer their research questions, because the plans contained little information about the teachers' approach to literacy instruction. With this piece of teacher input no longer included, the team decided to send out a survey to teachers instead of just one email prompt. This way, the researchers would get more information about teachers' practices. The team sent the survey using Google Forms and decided to have teachers not include identifying information (see resource J for an example).

The group responsible for developing the fieldnote instrument wanted the observation to be as open-ended as possible to get a range of perspectives and experiences, as everyone on the research team might have a different understanding of what literacy looks like, and the smaller group did not want to limit these observations. The small group decided that after the first open observation, everyone would share his or her fieldnotes and write a brief memo about each other's fieldnotes. The team would then conduct another, more focused observation when all the team members had a shared definition of literacy practices and of what they were looking for in the observations.

Because Charles and his team divided the tasks of data collection, they finished collecting data in two months. The team also employed many of the collaborative research mindsets discussed in the previous chapter. These included a recognition of the importance of multiple perspectives, a commitment to shared learning through collaborative research, and an openness to change.

COLLECTING VALID DATA

Chapter 3 defined four processes that help ensure the validity of your research studies: participant validation, the inclusion of multiple perspectives and data sources, reflexivity, and dialogic engagement. We review the definitions of these validity processes in table 5.3 for your reference. In this section, we present an example of how an applied research team used these validity processes while collecting data.

Participant Validation

Tamika, a superintendent for a large urban school district on the West Coast, decided that there was a need to study principal fidelity in implementing district initiatives. She asked two principals to help her choose the remaining members of the applied research team, which ultimately included two colleagues in the district central office, a member of the school board, the two principals, and two teachers. Part of the team's research design plan was to interview principals about how initiatives were communicated to them, how much and what kinds of support they received for the implementation of the initiatives, and what, if any, follow-up was done to see how each principal and school adopted

TABLE 5.3 Validity processes for applied research

VALIDITY PROCESS	DEFINITION
Participant validation	Checking in with participants to get feedback on your research design, methods, instruments, analysis, and interpretations will increase the study's validity.
Multiple perspectives and data sources	Including multiple perspectives on your research team and in the pool of study participants promotes study validity by showing that you value perspectives and experiences different from your own. Comparing different sources of data (e.g., observations, interviews, preexisting data, and focus groups) is another way to make a study more valid.
Reflexivity	Critically reflecting how you (and your team members) influence the research process, and monitoring and addressing that influence, can increase the validity of your study.
Dialogic engagement	Deliberately engaging with others to review your research processes, including the instruments, methods, and interpretations, is essential to having a more valid study.

the new initiatives. The team developed an interview instrument to use with twenty principals in the district. The aim was to select a range of principals from schools of different types and locations throughout the district.

After conducting individual interviews with three of the twenty principals, the team members scheduled thirty-minute discussion sessions (participant validation) in which they could check in with these three principals to discuss the interview process and ask for feedback on the interview questions as well. After this validation step, Tamika and her team reworded several of their interview questions so that they were clearer and contained less jargon, since two of the principals commented that several questions were awkwardly worded and included very specific terminology. In addition, talking to principals helped the team rethink the order of the questions so that they flowed better. Finally, these check-ins also let Tamika and the team know that they needed to clearly frame this research as informational and not as evaluative since all three principals said that they felt somewhat concerned that they were being evaluated on their responses. Given the feedback during this early participant validation, Tamika decided to inform all twenty principals that the research process and findings would be used to directly improve district practices to support principals rather than as part of their performance review. Communicating this clearly at the outset was very important to address potential concerns principals may have about how the data would be used and to get more honest answers.

Participant validation can be scheduled at any point or at several points during a project. The validation step we discussed in this example relates to preliminary data analysis. It was conducted to improve the team's data collection tools. By checking in with participants, the team learned that it needed to share with the other principals the nature of the research and assure them that the research was not evaluative and hence would not affect them negatively.

To further refine the research instruments, you can conduct participant validation while you are still collecting data. Participant validation can also be conducted when all data have been collected to elicit the participants' opinions about findings or action plans. The goal across any kind of participant validation is to ask the participants to share their ideas and experiences about the research topic and process. Furthermore, the validation step can be considered a form of data since it often consists of very focused follow-up conversations. If participant validation will also be used for these purposes, it should be recorded and careful notes should be taken during these sessions.

Multiple Perspectives and Data Sources

Tamika and the other members of the research team knew that they could not rely only on interviews with principals to answer their research questions. After checking in with the first three principals, the team decided to conduct additional interviews with teachers at the schools of the principals they had interviewed. The goal was to see if and how teachers learned about district initiatives. Tamika understood the value and importance of including numerous perspectives when she assembled her research team, and given how generative this diversity was, Tamika and the team decided that they needed to carry this variety of perspectives into their data collection. To seek out diversity in their data, they strategically selected people with various perspectives to help them answer their research questions. The team members interviewed a range of teachers, conducted two focus groups with assistant principals, and engaged in observation at an all-principal professional development session related to the district initiative.

Furthermore, the members reviewed the many documents that the district gave to principals to introduce and support the initiative. These documents included introductory material, progress updates, supporting materials, requests for specific kinds of data from the principals, faculty professional development materials related to the initiative, and so forth. To better understand how these materials were used, the team brought copies of them to the principal interviews and asked the principals how they used and understood these documents. The team then asked the assistant principals the same questions. In this way, Tamika and her research team gathered multiple perspectives (principals, assistant principals, and teachers) and data sources (interviews, focus groups, fieldnotes, and review of preexisting data) to help make their research as valid as possible.

Reflexivity

Tamika knew that having the research team members reflect on their biases and potential blind spots as a formal step at the beginning of the research would help the team become aware of how these biases could influence the research. Furthermore, she wanted to proactively avoid any defensiveness by the members if the principals said they were not adequately supported by the district when a new initiative started. Thus, Tamika developed a streamlined process for writing what she called *mini memos*. During every other team meeting, she and her team composed these mini memos in which they reflected on how aspects of their identities, beliefs, biases, and so on, could affect the research.

The first fifteen minutes of these alternate team meetings were dedicated to these mini memos. Tamika structured these sessions by writing three topics or prompts for the team members to choose from and respond to during this time. The prompts were specific to the research process in which the team was currently engaged. Here is one set of prompts she used:

1. While engaging with participants, how have I presumed shared identity? What did this look like, and what impact did it (or could it) have on the data?
2. Describe expectations you had during an interview, focus group, or observation. How are these expectations related to your identity, biases, and other beliefs?
3. During an interview or a focus group, have you been surprised about how a participant responded? What do you think underlay that surprise?

By trying to uncover the biases that people bring into research, these prompts aim to create a team dynamic where these issues are systematically and openly discussed. At the end of the fifteen-minute reflection, the team members were allotted ten minutes to collaboratively discuss how they could address the issues that they had noted in the memos. In this way, the team documented how they might be responding to or influencing the research, and then the team collaboratively problem-solved ways to monitor these influences.

The team continued writing mini memos throughout the remainder of the project. Many team members said that these memos helped them focus at the outset of meetings and made the discussions more specific and therefore effective. They also said that the exercise created a kind of group accountability by having the members reflect on their own "baggage" and how this baggage could cloud their vision and shape their interpretations in potentially problematic ways in the research. Mini memos are one way of engaging in team reflexivity, but there are many other ways. The leaders we work with have said that having the team come up with ideas for mini memo topics and other kinds of reflexive writing and dialogue is useful to the entire research process. It can help to have a few people assigned to keep these reflexive exercises on their radar and bring them back into the group for critical dialogue over time. As we discuss in chapter 6, engaging in reflexivity individually and as a group is vital to valid data analysis since biases and assumptions shape how we read and interpret data.

Dialogic Engagement

Tamika and her applied research team worked as a dialogic engagement group. They collaboratively discussed, problem-solved, and reviewed the group's research processes. Specifically, during data collection, through dialogic engagement, the team refined its interview instruments and determined which preexisting data it would review. The team also shared data collection memos that were used as a part of **formative data analysis,** which refers to processes of analyzing data throughout a study (as opposed to just at its end). For example, after conducting several interviews with principals and teachers, all the team members wrote their own memos in which they described (1) the data they had collected so far, (2) what they were learning, (3) what potential themes they were seeing in the data, and (4) what was surprising about the data. The team members shared and discussed their memos with each other at several meetings, and notes were taken during the discussions.

Because the memos were composed while the team was still collecting data, the members could decide if they needed to collect additional data. For example, Tamika and her team decided to conduct a focus group with district staff members to better understand how district officials supported the principals during new initiatives. And by engaging in ongoing dialogue about data collection, the team came up with new ideas, including the use of an email prompt to participants to quickly gather additional data on one or two specific questions.

PRACTICES TO START

Here are some useful practices to help you and your team members start collecting actionable data. These practices include a data collection plan and timeline, ways to align your methods and research questions, reflexive data collection activities, and instrument refinement exercises.

PRACTICE 12: *Data Collection Plan and Timeline*

Collectively developing a data collection plan and timeline is important for many reasons. First, the plan will detail the different tasks of data collection, the individuals responsible for completing them, and the dates when the tasks should be completed. Second, creating this plan and setting a realistic timeline will help you and your team strategically conduct the research. In resource K, we include an example of a data collection plan that one team developed. There are many additional ways to create a plan, but several aspects of its development are important:

- Team members should brainstorm the many research-related tasks that they need to accomplish.
- These tasks should be divided among team members.
- The team needs to agree on reasonable dates.
- Validity processes should be built into the timeline.
- Formative data analysis processes should also be built into the timeline.
- There is flexibility for refinement and changes.
- The team must have a sense of how all the data they need will be collected.

PRACTICE 13: *Aligning Data Collection Methods with Research Questions*

We have stressed the importance of how methods should be directly related to your research questions. To help you and your team make sure your methods align with your research questions, we recommend that you and your team review resource L. Your team can collectively fill in this form during one or two meetings so that people are a part of the development process; this collaboration promotes greater ownership and a clearer path forward. Furthermore, engaging in these discussions can help you and your team determine if you are asking the right questions, how and if they need to be changed, and what methods will best help you answer your questions.

PRACTICE 14: *Reflexive Data Collection Through Mini Memos*

As described in this chapter, one way to practice reflexivity when you are collecting data is to write mini memos. These brief memos are written by research teams during meetings. You can structure your team's memo writing the way Tamika did with her team. For example, you could have the team members write their responses to a prompt in a whole-group setting and then discuss their impressions. A few sample memos could be related to the following topics:

- *Assumptions*: In this mini memo, people reflect on their working assumptions about the research topic, the expected findings, their expectations or what they think others expect from the research, and any other assumptions that would be valuable to uncover early in the research process. Sharing these mini memos about assumptions allows them to be discussed and challenged.
- *Ideas and concerns*: This mini memo can be written early on and in the middle of data collection so that people can share what they are learning about the topic and the research process. Discussing their memos as a group will allow the members to share their knowledge and to troubleshoot problems. This sharing will help refine the data collection process when the exercise is conducted around midway through the data collection. It can be repeated at the end of data collection as well.

PRACTICE 15: *Refining Research Instruments*

As data collection instruments are created, team members will want to have others review them (i.e., vet the instruments) and practice using them (i.e., rehearse and pilot the instruments). We suggest different ways that applied research team members can vet, rehearse, and pilot data collection instruments.

Vetting

After the team has come up with a working set of questions for interviews, focus groups, or surveys, the team members take a printed or email version of the instrument and vet it by others in their circles (to be determined as a group). Team members then come back together as a team and share the feedback. Projecting the instrument on a screen can be useful during this session so that members can more easily make changes as a group.

Rehearsing

Rehearsing conducting an interview or a focus group can help team members become familiar with the questions, potential responses, and flow of the session. One way to rehearse is to work in pairs for interviews and in small groups for focus groups and to take turns going through the entire instrument, including the introduction, asking each question out loud and hearing responses (even though they are fictitious), taking notes, and timing how long the interview or focus group lasts. Ask your partner or group for focused feedback on the wording and flow of questions and if anything is missing or problematic. Also ask about your style and approach (e.g., do you reword questions too quickly, do you interrupt, do you seem anxious or unclear?). Discuss together if the questions make sense and seem to elicit the information needed to answer the research questions. Also note how long the questions take individually and as a whole. After rehearsing the instruments, you'll want to discuss as an entire team how the rehearsals went and then make changes.

Piloting

When your team pilots an instrument, the members choose a few participants who fit the descriptions created for relevant stakeholder groups and go through the interview with these people. The team then records the participants' responses. These pilot processes may help refine the instruments since they are conducted with actual participants. Sometimes, these participants will be interviewed again. Other times, the pilot interviews, if not changed dramatically, can be included as formal data. At still other times, if the instruments change considerably, the pilot interviews may not be included in the data set at all.

Fishbowl Exercises

Across our work with applied research teams, we have seen that it can be productive for team members with strong interviewing and focus group facilitation skills to model their approach and share their skills with the rest of the team. In a fishbowl exercise, people in the physical center of a group are engaging in an activity carefully observed by those seated in the periphery. These observers take notes and ask questions throughout. This exercise is an excellent form of professional development and a useful way to raise the quality of the data by improving both the teams' collective research skills and, consequently, the validity of the interviews and focus groups.

For these fishbowl exercises, we suggest using the actual instruments when doing the mock interview or focus group, with some team members designated as interviewees. During the exercise, have the facilitating team member share process-oriented comments and tips. Observers should take fieldnotes, which gives the team the experience of practicing that skill as well. Furthermore, set the fishbowl up in a way that allows team members to stop the interview or focus group and ask questions in the moment. Fishbowl exercises are valuable since people can learn together how to conduct effective interviews and focus groups, how to take notes unobtrusively, and other related process and facilitation skills. Hearing each other's questions is useful and can generate a group understanding and shared research lexicon.

CHAPTER SUMMARY

We began this chapter with a discussion about how research questions are central in applied research. We then described primary data collection methods, including interviews, focus groups, fieldnotes, surveys, photovoice, and mapping. For a majority of these methods, we included and referred readers to multiple examples of instruments in the resources section at the end of the book. This chapter also continued the discussion of how Charles and his team studied their school's approach to literacy instruction, and it detailed their data collection processes. We also looked at how validity processes are used in data collection, presenting an example of how a superintendent, Tamika, used participant validation, multiple perspectives and data sources, systematic reflexivity, and dialogic engagement to make their study as valid as possible. The chapter concluded by detailing four practices to help you and your research team collect valid and actionable data: developing a plan and timeline for data collection, aligning data collection methods with research questions, creating mini memos, and refining and rehearsing your data collection instruments.

SIX

Conducting Data Analysis

WE BEGIN THIS CHAPTER by introducing data analysis and discussing its central principles. We then detail three data analysis processes for applied research: recording and organizing data, formative data analysis, and summative analysis. After describing these three processes, we show how to collaboratively develop thematic findings. Throughout this chapter, we present tips and examples of what data analysis processes look like. In addition, we include a detailed example of how one applied research team analyzed its data and developed actionable findings. The chapter concludes with two practices to help you and your team get started analyzing data.

Throughout this chapter, we address the following questions:

- What is data analysis?
- What does data analysis involve?
- How can you and your team plan to record and organize data?
- What is formative analysis and its related processes?
- What is **coding**? How does your team code your data?
- What are some ways to analyze qualitative data in relation to preexisting data?
- What are important considerations when you are developing thematic findings?

OVERVIEW OF DATA ANALYSIS

Data analysis refers to intentional ways of making sense of data. In this book, our discussion of data analysis focuses solely on qualitative data analysis. Qualitative data analysis in applied research is an iterative process. Like applied research in general, data analysis processes change over time in light of the researchers' evolving understanding of the data collected. This approach is called formative data analysis (see chapter 5): as soon as you begin collecting data, you are starting to make sense of, and analyze, your data in a preliminary way. Data analysis also involves summative data analysis processes, which are conducted once all your data are collected.[1] When you analyze qualitative data, you are interpreting other people's experiences, and you are thus ethically responsible for faithfully and respectfully representing what you are learning. (In so doing, you must also challenge your biases and assumptions.) We present these guiding principles of strategic and systematic data analysis for you to keep in mind throughout the analytical processes.

- Data analysis is closely and consistently aligned with your research questions.
- The analysis starts as soon as the first piece of data is collected.
- Data can be organized and themes can be described through the use of memos.
- You and your team use analytic memos that can directly inform your findings.

Throughout this chapter, we discuss specific strategies and methods for analyzing data.

DATA ANALYSIS PROCESSES

As we have described, in applied research studies, there are three essential data analysis processes: (1) recording and organizing the data to facilitate analysis, (2) formative data analysis to capture what you are learning, and (3) summative

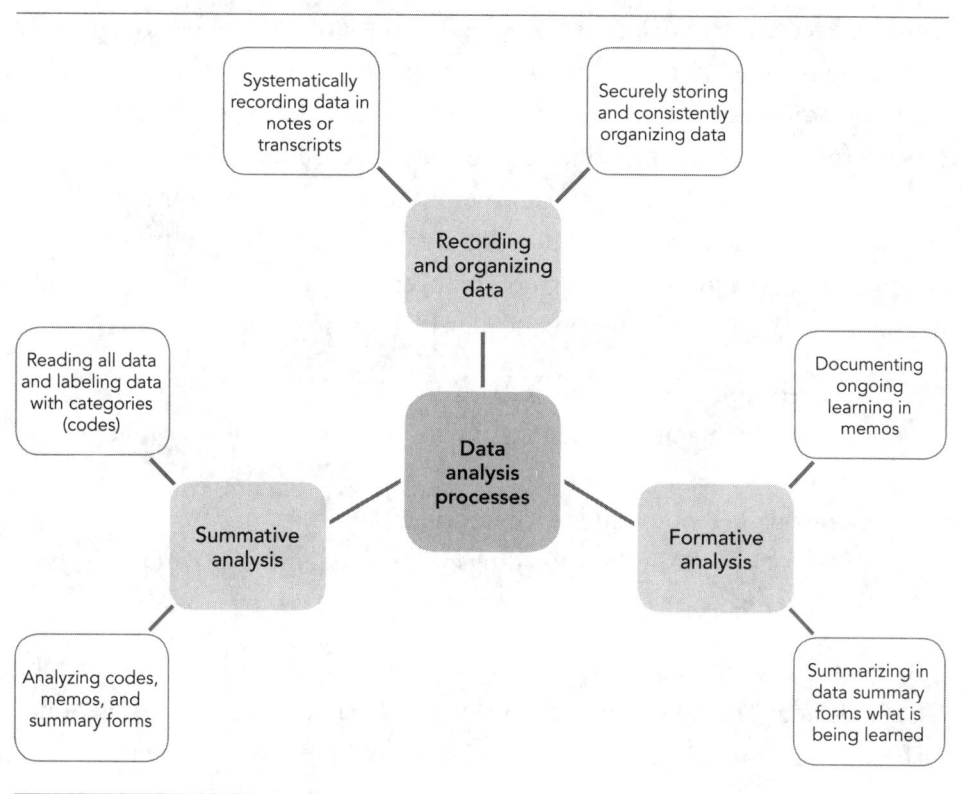

FIGURE 6.1 Data analysis processes

Data analysis processes (center), connected to four surrounding nodes:
- **Recording and organizing data**: Systematically recording data in notes or transcripts; Securely storing and consistently organizing data
- **Formative analysis**: Documenting ongoing learning in memos; Summarizing in data summary forms what is being learned
- **Summative analysis**: Reading all data and labeling data with categories (codes); Analyzing codes, memos, and summary forms

analysis of the entire data set once all the data have been collected (figure 6.1). We discuss each of these processes in the following sections.

Recording and Organizing Data

For effective data analysis, you and your team should have a plan for how your data will be recorded and organized. For example, will they be audio-recorded and transcribed or captured in notes? And where and how will they be stored? Your team needs a plan in place *before* you begin data collection. Otherwise, data can be lost or hard to find at a later date. We'll discuss each of these important processes of recording and organizing data in turn.

How are people's spoken words recorded so that they become data? The words are recorded in two primary ways, by transcribing audio-recordings or by writing detailed notes. There are pros and cons to each method. Turning audio-recordings into transcripts can be a time-consuming or expensive process. In resource M, we describe several useful transcription services or software available to your team. When you rely solely on notes, some aspects of an interview or event are inevitably forgotten or missed. From our experience conducting applied research in schools for over a decade, we think that the best option for recording data for school teams involves the following steps:

- Audio-record all data collected.
- Collect the data in pairs so that one person can take notes while the other facilitates.
- Write detailed notes after each interview and focus group.
- Refer back to the audio-recordings when needed (e.g., to quote participants).

These four steps help school teams to sufficiently capture all the data they have collected. The audio-recordings act as a backup in case notes were not taken (or if they are illegible, lost, etc.). If you have additional time or finances, we recommend that all audio-recordings be transcribed. If you go this route, you do not need to have two researchers at every interview or focus group.

There are many ways to organize and store data. Because you are working with a team, you should, among other things, make sure that everyone can easily access the data and find all the related files. You also need to make sure that the data are securely stored. Many research teams use a password-protected online portal (e.g., Dropbox, Box, or a school-specific platform like Canvas) for storing and sharing data. Regardless of what platform you use, it is a best practice to remove identifying information from data (e.g., substitute participants' names with pseudonyms) before you upload the information to a shared portal or platform. In addition to determining where you will store the data, you may consider developing a shared system for labeling and organizing files consistently. When working on a research team, you need to consider these matters of file management to make sure that the data can be easily retrieved by all the members of the team. For example, after taking notes during an interview, a team member should save these notes and upload them to a place where all the other members can access them. To help team members access the data, you should name the files consistently (e.g., according to date and type of data) and place the document in an appropriately named folder. Table 6.1 presents considerations for organizing and storing your data.

Formative Data Analysis

Formative data analysis refers to proactive analysis processes that happen while data are still being collected. These early analysis processes are often captured in **researcher memos** and **data summary forms** and then are discussed in team meetings. You need to document these formative analysis processes as systematically as possible, as they provide insight into what you are learning about a topic. Formative analysis can also help you and your research team determine whether you need to revise your data collection instruments and gather additional data. For the remainder of this section, we detail how to capture the knowledge generated through different methods of formative data analysis and discussion.

TABLE 6.1 Considerations for organizing and storing data

- Where will your data be stored (e.g., Dropbox, locked file cabinet in a secure room, Canvas)?
- How will team members access the data files?
- How will the data be protected? That is, how will access be restricted?
- How will the files be labeled? What will be included in the file label, and in what order?
- How will you label your folders for organizing the data?
- Do these folder names and organizational system make sense to team members so that they can easily upload information to the correct folder?
- What relevant information will be listed at the top of a file (e.g., date of the interview, interviewer or interviewers, time, location, name of the participant or pseudonym)?
- Will the identifying information be removed from the data before a file is uploaded to a portal?
- Are pages numbered consistently across all data sources?

Researcher Memos

Formative data analysis memos are a useful and efficient way for you and your team members, as researchers, to document what you are learning during data collection, to discuss potential concerns or other issues, and to decide on your next steps for data collection and analysis. These memos should be shared with members of your team and then stored and organized along with the rest of your data, as they will be referred to throughout the data analysis process. Having team members prepare a short memo before each meeting is a great way to focus the team's efforts. These topics can also be structured as mini memos, in which everyone writes down his or her ideas during the meeting (see chapter 5).

As we have noted, these memos can be written about many issues. For example, in discussing some important ideas about the data, you might consider the following prompts:

- What stands out to you after a few interviews or observations or after you have collected some other data?
- Include excerpts of data (e.g., quotes or fieldnotes), and explain why you included these excerpts. What are you learning from these pieces of data?
- How do these excerpts compare with other data collected?
- What are your next steps for data collection and analysis? (For example, you might want to follow up with a specific participant, conduct additional observations, or make a change to your interview instrument.)

Other helpful questions to consider in these memos include asking what or who might be missing from your data and what has surprised you about the data you have collected so far. When discussing what surprised you, you might want to include concrete examples from your data.

Finally, formative data analysis memos are also a good place to document any potential themes you are starting to see in your data. You might describe what the potential themes are, what they tell you, how they relate to the research questions and goals of the applied research, and examples of how the data illustrate this theme.

The topics and questions we suggest here are a starting point as you begin to analyze your data and write formative analysis memos. You can include any combination of these topics or questions as you write these memos. We also recommend that you share and discuss these memos with your team members.

Data Summary Forms

Data summary forms record the research team's notes directly after the members have collected data. For example, after conducting an interview, you will fill out a data summary form that highlights key aspects of the interview, suggests potential themes that came up, and notes questions to ask a different participant or another team member. These summary forms are especially important when you are conducting applied research with teams, as the forms help team members who were not present at the interview, focus group, or observation to get a sense of what was learned. Furthermore, these forms are a way of engaging in formative analysis as you continue to collect data.

Data summary forms can also be used for summarizing findings from pre-existing (archival data) or quantitative data such as test scores or attendance data. For example, if a team member reviewed the school code of conduct, he or she could fill out a data summary form to share the information with other team members. By summarizing preexisting information in these data forms, you make sure that it becomes a part of the data that you will analyze.

In summary, storing and organizing all data, memos, and summary forms is important so that team members can easily access this information for review and share files with each other. Table 6.2 describes important information to include on a data summary form, and we present two examples of data summary forms in resource N.

Summative Analysis

There are many approaches to summative data analysis. The approach we present here is based on thematic analysis, which involves determining key findings that note similarities and differences in your data.[2] As represented in figure 6.2, this process involves (1) reading and coding (or labeling) all your

TABLE 6.2 Information included in data summary forms

- Type of data (e.g., preexisting information, interview, observation, focus group, survey, quantitative data)
- Person or persons involved (e.g., interviewer and interviewee)
- Date, time, and location of data collection
- Date when the summary form was completed
- Short summary of what was learned or occurred during data collection
- Questions remaining
- People to follow up with for more information
- Potential themes or codes that can be used to categorize the data
- Other notes or important ideas that surface

data; (2) analyzing the coded data, formative analysis memos, and data summary forms; and (3) documenting your learning in summative analysis memos. We detail each of these three steps in this section.

Reading and Coding All Your Data

A first step in summative data analysis, reading and coding your data, applies to all the relevant preexisting data that you reviewed (e.g., quantitative data such as test scores or other metrics) and the data you have collected. Before you and your team take this step, you want to keep your research questions in mind. Reconsider your goals and the audiences for your research: what are you looking for and hoping to learn from these data? This is when you turn to the formative analysis documents (e.g., formative data analysis memos and data summary forms) and your literature review to look for themes in your data.

As a team, you will want to agree on what all of you will be noting as you read the data. For example, you may develop ten to fifteen categories that everyone will use and understand. As you and the other members read the data, you will apply one or some of these categories to the information. These categories are also called *codes*, or tags, because as you read the data and see evidence of one or more of these categories, you code that piece of data by labeling it with the corresponding category or categories.

During this process, which is similar to the textual analysis you may have learned in high school or college English courses, it can be helpful to develop

FIGURE 6.2 Summative data analysis processes

Read and code all data → Analyze coded data, memos, and data summary forms → Compose summative analysis memos

definitions of these codes to help unify everyone's understanding. These definitions will help team members know when they should assign a code to a section of data. Resource O includes one example of a code list and its corresponding definitions.

There are many ways to develop codes. Some codes may come from scholarly literature, practice frameworks, or background knowledge. For example, if you and your team are studying team dynamics, some of your ideas for categories would come from your prior knowledge or the literature. You might come up with codes such as *distributed leadership*, *team norms*, and *handling conflict*. Broadly, codes that come from preexisting sources are called *deductive codes*. Other codes may come from your data summary forms or formative analysis memos. These codes might note aspects that you have noticed through formative analysis of your data or while reading your data. For example, you might come up with *peacemaker*, *strategies for bridging groups*, and *consensus building*. Codes that come directly from your data are referred to as *inductive codes*. Some codes may be a combination of inductive and deductive processes. Consensus building, for example, is discussed in literature about teams but is also something that the participants specifically mentioned in the data. When you and your team are developing codes that will help you make sense of your data, you must keep your research questions in mind.

After you have determined the codes that you and your team are going to use as you read the data, we recommend that you divide the data among team members so that every team member is assigned an amount of data to read and code. As team members read the data (e.g., a transcript, interview notes, or fieldnotes), every time an example of a code comes up, they will each highlight that piece of data and code it by attaching a label or notes to the piece of data.

Figure 6.3 demonstrates an example of coding data. The team member selected a portion of an interview transcript and labeled it with various codes (*students' interests*, *guided reading*, *differentiated instruction*, *critical thinking*, and *"right level"*) using a commenting feature. In this example, you can also see that more than one code can be applied to a portion of data, although some portions may have only one code.

A couple of things are worth noting in this example. The codes were collaboratively developed by the team in relation to their research question about the literacy practices in the school. All the codes applied in this example were determined by the team in advance except for the term *right level*. When the teacher brought up this idea in an interview, the researcher decided to note it in case it continued to occur in other interviews.

FIGURE 6.3   Example of coding

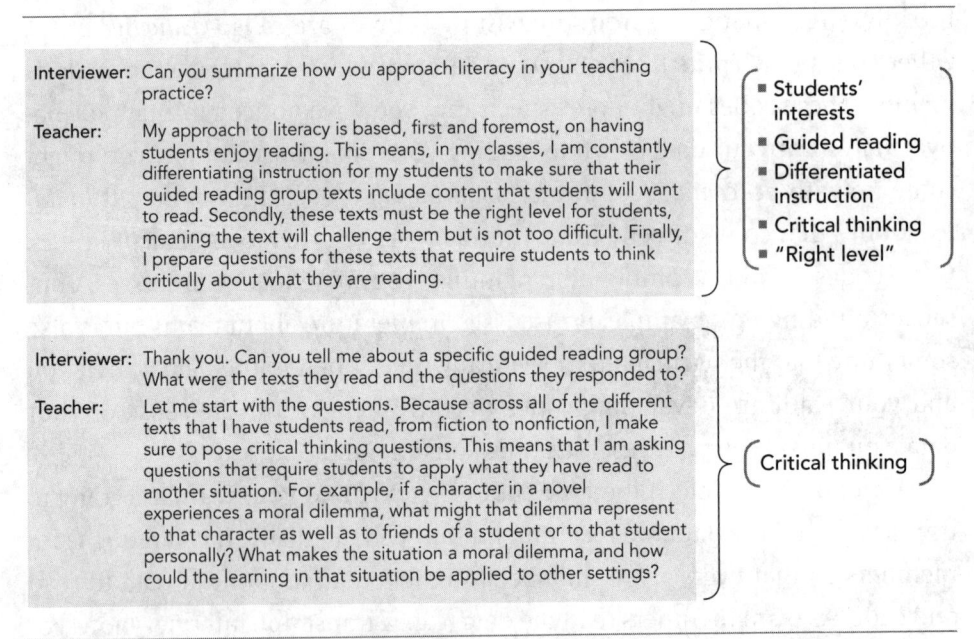

Interviewer: Can you summarize how you approach literacy in your teaching practice?

Teacher: My approach to literacy is based, first and foremost, on having students enjoy reading. This means, in my classes, I am constantly differentiating instruction for my students to make sure that their guided reading group texts include content that students will want to read. Secondly, these texts must be the right level for students, meaning the text will challenge them but is not too difficult. Finally, I prepare questions for these texts that require students to think critically about what they are reading.

- Students' interests
- Guided reading
- Differentiated instruction
- Critical thinking
- "Right level"

Interviewer: Thank you. Can you tell me about a specific guided reading group? What were the texts they read and the questions they responded to?

Teacher: Let me start with the questions. Because across all of the different texts that I have students read, from fiction to nonfiction, I make sure to pose critical thinking questions. This means that I am asking questions that require students to apply what they have read to another situation. For example, if a character in a novel experiences a moral dilemma, what might that dilemma represent to that character as well as to friends of a student or to that student personally? What makes the situation a moral dilemma, and how could the learning in that situation be applied to other settings?

Critical thinking

There are many other ways to code data, including color-coding or highlighting systems and coding by hand. There is no right or wrong way to code data. Coding is a tool that researchers use to make sense of their data. By itself, coding is not analysis. Rather, it is part of the analytic process. Furthermore, if you and your team come across a concept that you think is important but is not reflected in your codes, you can still note this idea and code it as something along the lines of "important but not in codes."

To review, there are three approaches to reading and coding all your data. The first is an **inductive analytical approach**, in which you look for emerging themes or patterns as you read the data or as you prepare formative analysis memos or data summary forms. The second is a **deductive analytical approach**, in which you see if external theories from an existing framework (e.g., a program's logic model or existing literature) are present in your data. The third approach is a combination of inductive and deductive analytical approaches; you are coding your data with both deductive codes coming from the literature or other predetermined concepts and inductive codes that you notice directly from the data.

Consider another example of a deductive analytical approach. Let's say your team is studying a topic related to child development. You could use an existing developmental framework, such as Urie Bronfenbrenner's ecological development model, to code your information. The data could be coded according to how they fit the model's systems (e.g., microsystems, meaning one's immediate surroundings, or mesosystems, consisting of interactions between microsystems) that affect an individual's development.[3] Figure 6.4 presents an example of the concurrent use of deductive codes (microsystem and mesosystem) and an inductive code (supports). In this figure, you can also see how different pieces of data can be coded with more than one code. Because coding data is a time-consuming task, you and your team will want to decide in advance which codes you will use to label your data. However, we recommend also remaining open to other concepts that come up as you read the data since a primary goal of the research is to learn from the participants' thoughts and experiences related to the topic.

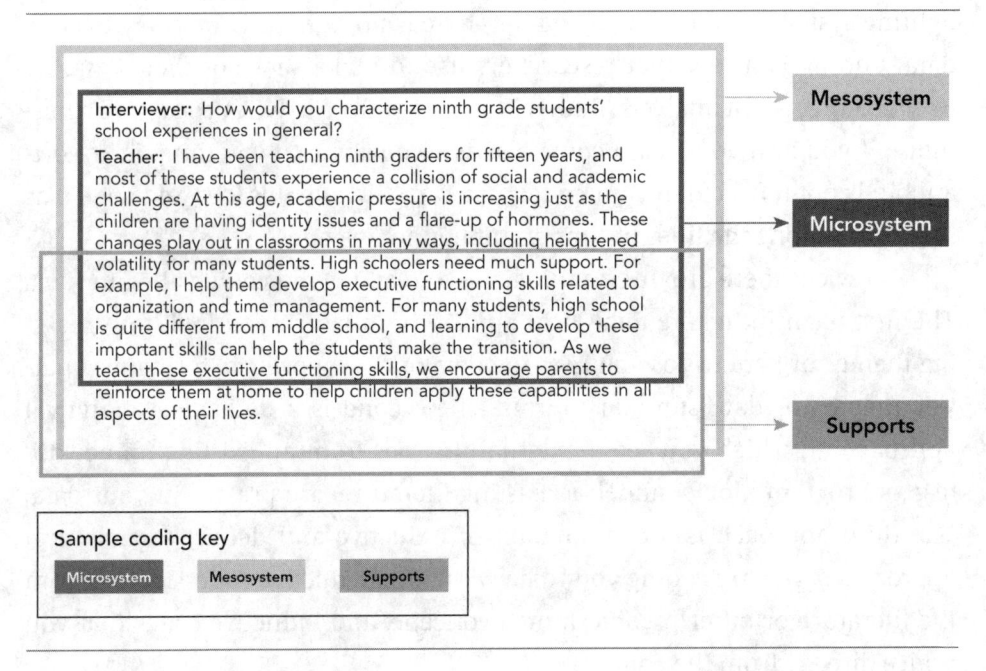

FIGURE 6.4 Example of deductive and inductive coding

Interviewer: How would you characterize ninth grade students' school experiences in general?

Teacher: I have been teaching ninth graders for fifteen years, and most of these students experience a collision of social and academic challenges. At this age, academic pressure is increasing just as the children are having identity issues and a flare-up of hormones. These changes play out in classrooms in many ways, including heightened volatility for many students. High schoolers need much support. For example, I help them develop executive functioning skills related to organization and time management. For many students, high school is quite different from middle school, and learning to develop these important skills can help the students make the transition. As we teach these executive functioning skills, we encourage parents to reinforce them at home to help children apply these capabilities in all aspects of their lives.

→ Mesosystem
→ Microsystem
→ Supports

Sample coding key: Microsystem | Mesosystem | Supports

All data, including preexisting data, can be coded. Coding and organizing your data are iterative processes, and it is common for codes to evolve. For example, codes often start out descriptive, simply describing something that is happening in interviews, focus groups, or other data-gathering instruments. As we discuss in the next section, codes often evolve into more analytical categories.

Analyzing Coded Data, Formative Analysis Memos, and Data Summary Forms

The second step in summative analysis is analyzing your coded data, memos, and data summary forms. To begin this analysis, you should first organize your coded data. There are many ways to do this, including creating a separate Word document for each code or organizing the coded data in a spreadsheet (table 6.3). In the table, you can see how the team started organizing its data for

TABLE 6.3 An example of organizing coded data

CODE	DATA SOURCE	DATA EXCERPT
Critical thinking	Interview transcript	*Interviewer:* Can you summarize how you approach literacy in your teaching practice? *Teacher 1:* My approach to literacy is based primarily on having students enjoy reading. This means that in my classes, I am constantly differentiating instruction for my students to make sure that their guided reading group texts include content that students will want to read . . . Finally, I prepare questions for these texts that require students to think critically about what they are reading.
Critical thinking	Interview transcript	*Interviewer:* Thank you. Can you tell me about a specific guided reading group? What texts did they read, and which questions did they respond to? *Teacher 2:* Let me start with the questions. Because across all the different texts that I have students read, from fiction to nonfiction, I make sure to pose critical-thinking questions. This means that I'm asking questions that require students to apply what they have read to another situation. For example, if a character in a novel experiences a moral dilemma, what might that dilemma represent to that character, to the student, or to the student's friends?
Critical thinking	Teacher survey	My approach to literacy is embedded in my practice primarily in how I approach what literacy means. I think about literacy as a way to expand students' horizons, as a way for them to question, challenge, and think about the world. In this regard, I embed literacy in everything I teach. When teaching social studies, I do not focus on asking students to recall facts. Instead, I ask them to engage in what various concepts mean. In this regard, I am teaching them to "read the world," so to speak. How can we make sense of what is going on around? That is how I approach literacy. (*Teacher 5*)
Critical thinking	Literacy assessment (preexisting data)	9. Why did Marcus choose to return the gift? In your answer, explain the dilemma that he was facing and why he did what he did. Include evidence from the text as you discuss Marcus's decision-making and the problem he solved. 10. What would you have done if you were in Marcus's position? Explain how you would have responded to the dilemma and what your reasons for doing so would include. (*Teacher 2 created this assessment*)
Critical thinking	Fieldnotes	Students are responding to an open-ended prompt to describe how they would have responded to an event that a character experienced in the novel the class is reading. Students write individually for a few minutes and then share with a partner. During their partner discussion, students are asked to cite from the novel the evidence that informs their decisions. During these partner discussions, Ms. Donaldson checks in and listens to a majority of the partner groups. The class then comes back together, and Ms. Donaldson begins a whole-group discussion, hearing from different students. She encourages students to talk to each other and ask questions. (*Observation of Ms. Donaldson*)

each code. All the data that were assigned the code *critical thinking* were pulled out so that the researchers could see the different ways that critical thinking was discussed in interviews, surveys, assessment data, and observations. This example is an abbreviated version, as there were many more data excerpts that were coded critical thinking.

As you begin to organize your coded data, you might notice the quantity of data that has been assigned to each code. Which codes have many data excerpts assigned to them? Which have few? Are all the data coming from the same person? It is important to see if and how codes vary according to different participants. Did most participants discuss this concept, or did one participant discuss this concept at length? Some of the teams we have worked with assign a different color to each participant so that they can easily see where the data are coming from. Other teams make sure to clearly label each data excerpt with who said the quote (see, for example, table 6.3).

After organizing your coded data, you and the other team members will reread the data grouped by code. You should also reread the formative analysis memos and the data summary forms. For this part of the analysis, your team can decide to have everyone reread all the material or create subgroups that will review different parts of the material. As you read the organized coded data, you will probably begin to see whether some codes need to change and how some codes can be combined to create a new category. Some data may need to be recoded to more accurately reflect overall themes. Other codes may either be deleted or be rolled into another code. For instance, Charles and his team combined the codes *students' interests* and *welcoming environment* to create a new code of *student-centered learning*. Students' interests and *welcoming environment* were more descriptive codes in that they were describing things teachers discussed or did in their literacy classes. The new code, *student-centered learning*, is a more analytical code. It includes the description of what teachers are doing and saying as well as the way the team is analyzing or making sense of what these actions mean and what the team is learning about literacy instruction. In addition to changing, refining, or grouping codes, as team members read the coded data, formative analysis memos, and data summary forms, they will also want to look for potential patterns in what they are learning. The team can then document this learning in summative analysis memos, which we discuss in the next section.

Documenting Your Learning in Data Analysis Memos

In the final step of summative analysis, you and your group look at how you are making sense of the data. As you read your codes and formative analysis documents, you should notice the concepts that stand out, any salient quotes, and any other relevant data excerpts. We recommend then capturing your interpretations in a *summative analysis memo*. In this memo, you'll write about what you're learning from your data, the themes that you have developed and are developing, and the other ways the data could be interpreted.

The themes can sometimes include a combination of codes, but they do not have to be worded the same as the codes. Rather, they can relate to your codes thematically. That is, themes have a broader meaning and import than does a single code or concept. For example, *student-centered learning* discussed in the previous section is a theme that the team is using to make sense of the data. As another example, one team that was studying student behavior discussed in a summative data analysis memo how the codes *students skipping class* and *students talking back to teachers*, which were largely descriptive codes, were developed into the theme *student resistance*.

In the summative analysis memo, the team studying student behavior discussed how the original codes of *students skipping class* and *students talking back to teachers* were actually about ways that students resist oppressive structures. Thus, in this memo, the team included data excerpts that support their interpretation of the more analytical code of *student resistance*. At this stage of analysis, the team was moving from describing these data to interpreting them. For its next step, the group shared its summative analysis memo with the other members of the team to get feedback on the group's interpretations and on other ways that the data might be interpreted as the whole team is collectively making sense of the data. As you individually or collectively compose summative analysis memos, we recommend that you also work toward moving from descriptive to analytical themes.

In the summative analysis memo, explain what each theme means, and include two or three data excerpts that help explain this theme. The goal of this memo is to help you and your team make sense of all your data, and since the data were divided among team members, you need to share and discuss these memos with the whole team. Thus, this memo is a place where you can document patterns, themes, and potential discrepancies you see in your data. As you write these memos, you should collectively decide on their length. To get started on discussing themes, you might address some of the following:

- What themes do you see across the data that you read and coded?
- Describe the themes.
- How do these themes relate to the guiding research questions?
- Provide evidence, in the form of data excerpts, that illustrates each theme.
- Explain how each theme connects to, or differs from, the rest of the data.

In addition to discussing themes, you might also consider alternative explanations and interpretations that could apply to the themes and data and how you reconcile (or do not reconcile) your interpretations. After the team members have shared and collaboratively discussed their summative analysis memos with each other, they will begin to develop findings based on their research.

DEVELOPING FINDINGS

In a thematic approach to data analysis, the team develops primary themes that become the research findings. What differentiates themes from findings is that not every theme becomes a finding. Findings are analytic themes that relate to your research questions and are supported by your data. The number of findings you will have can vary, but the school leaders we have worked with say that three is often a good number. Two findings, they say, can become comparative, but more than three can dilute the significance of each finding. In this section, we describe the collaborative processes that help your team develop analytic findings: (1) sharing and discussing summative data analysis memos, (2) supporting the themes through data, and (3) situating your analytic themes and findings in relevant contexts, including the local setting and the context of all the data collected.

To develop findings, everyone on the team must first read and then discuss each other's summative analysis memos (see practice 17 at the end of this chapter). During these discussions, at least one team member should take detailed notes and all the members should discuss and then compare their memos and the central themes across the data. For example, in summative data analysis memos, team members might discuss patterns that they are noticing across the data and how their analysis of the coded data has helped them see analytic themes. Thus, in these whole-team meetings, everyone will discuss, debate, and examine analytic themes and other patterns they found in the data. It may take a couple of meetings for a team to agree on what the final findings for study include.

Developing thematic findings means that you and your team members present the information that you have learned from carefully and collectively analyzing your data. Thus, your findings represent that you have analyzed and interpreted your data and considered background knowledge and other contextual information. Analysis means more than paraphrasing your data or simply presenting data excerpts. It means that you and your team members present thematic, analytical findings and then support these findings with data excerpts that you explain. One way you and your team can make better sense of your data is by developing data displays, which are a way of synthesizing information to help you draw conclusions.[4] Figure 6.5 shows one data display that Charles and his team developed to help them make sense of what they were learning about students' and teachers' understanding of literacy practices.

As a part of discussing summative analysis memos, members of Charles's team began to sketch out in this data display what they thought they were

FIGURE 6.5   Example data analysis display

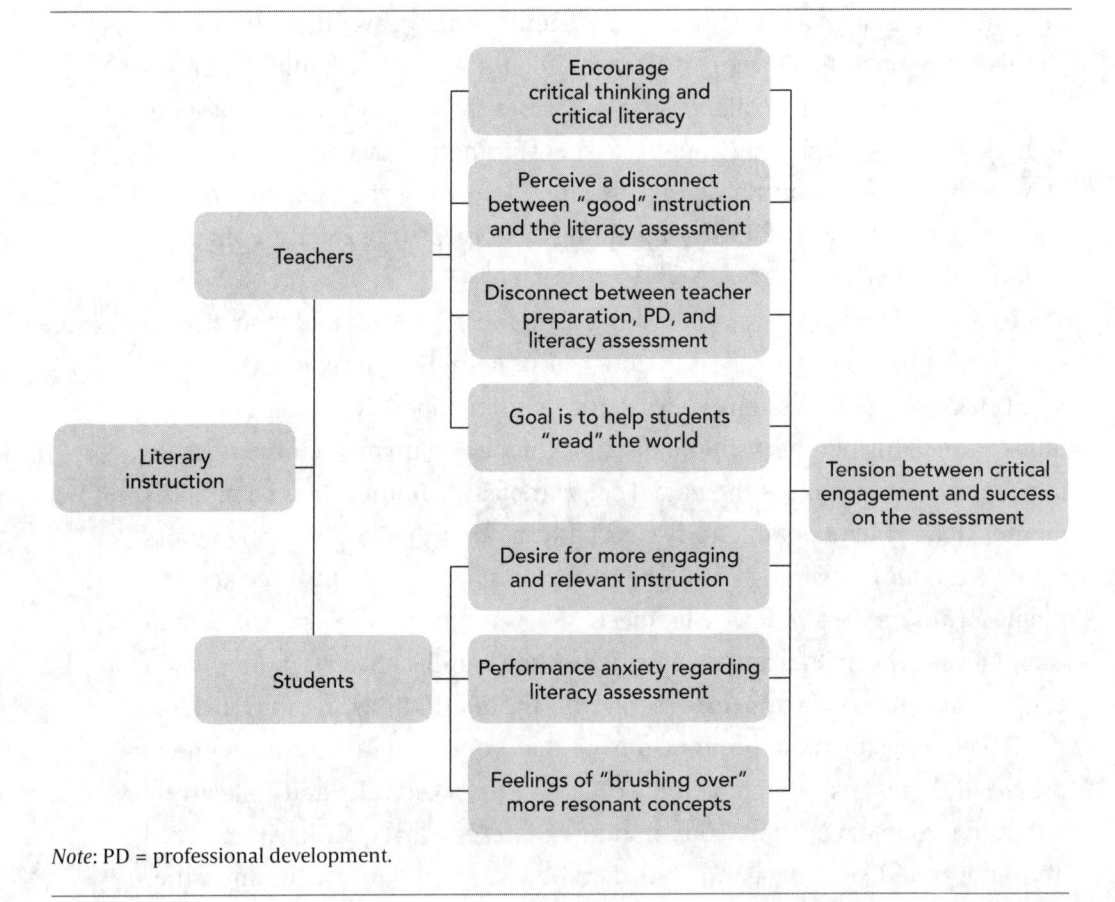

```
                            ┌─ Encourage critical thinking and critical literacy
                            │
                            ├─ Perceive a disconnect between "good" instruction
                            │  and the literacy assessment
              ┌─ Teachers ──┤
              │             ├─ Disconnect between teacher preparation, PD, and
              │             │  literacy assessment
              │             │
              │             └─ Goal is to help students "read" the world
Literary ─────┤                                                                   ─── Tension between critical
instruction   │                                                                       engagement and success
              │             ┌─ Desire for more engaging and relevant instruction      on the assessment
              │             │
              └─ Students ──┼─ Performance anxiety regarding literacy assessment
                            │
                            └─ Feelings of "brushing over" more resonant concepts
```

Note: PD = professional development.

learning from part of their data. The team's memos discussed teachers' and students' perceptions of literacy practices at the school. As you see in the figure, there are four themes related to the teachers' understanding of literacy instruction and three themes related to the students' experiences. Analysis of all these aspects led the team to develop a preliminary finding: that both students and teachers experience a conflict between critical engagement in the content and the pressure to succeed on the state assessment. As the data display shows, this finding is supported by the experiences of students and teachers in relationship to literacy instruction. The students expressed a desire for more engaging and relevant instruction, and teachers saw a disconnect between "good" instruction and what the test assesses.

The team members further refined this finding in their next team meeting to make the finding more contextually relevant to the school and to connect it to other parts of their data. Nevertheless, the process of developing a data display helped them progress in their analysis. The development of thematic findings is an iterative process, and the repetition can be frustrating at times, but it is also part of what helps create findings that are useful, relevant, and therefore actionable.

To review a few key points, codes can become, but do not necessarily become, findings. Your team may start out with ten to fifteen codes. By reading and coding the data, you may add a few more codes. Then, when the coded data are organized and discussed, you begin to see that some codes connect with one another and that many codes may be combined or deleted. Throughout this process, you are developing analytic themes that represent what you are learning in your data. You then discuss and document these themes in summative data analysis memos. These memos are shared and discussed by the entire team to unearth the primary themes that everyone notices in the data and to discover if any themes may have been left out. During these team meetings, you are working to combine and narrow the themes into approximately three thematic findings. Each thematic finding can, and often does, have subthemes that help support and explain it and is supported by evidence—in this case, your data.

Your thematic findings should relate to each other, and some findings may build off each other.[5] When you support your findings with data, you will want to explain these data excerpts. Because data do not speak for themselves, you will need to explain how the data relate to a theme. For example, if you are discussing the theme of student resistance and you include a quote from a student about why he or she skipped certain classes, you need to explain (1) what you mean by student resistance and (2) how this quote provides evidence of student resistance. Quotes are chosen because they are emblematic of a theme, and so this connection should be explicitly stated.

As you develop your findings, you will also want to connect them to your research questions, the local setting, and the background knowledge you reviewed at the outset of the study. For example, as you discuss the thematic finding of student resistance, you'll want to describe the context of your school and the grades (if relevant) to which you are referring. It can also be helpful to discuss what scholars or practitioners have written about student resistance and how this compares or differs and thus contextualizes your finding. As you and your team members progress in the development of thematic findings, it's okay to refine and reword your themes to make them more precise and clear. For example, the themes worded as "student disengagement" and "students negatively respond to uncritical pedagogical style and content" could be combined in this way so that the finding is more integrated and inclusive: "students base their level of engagement on how responsive and relevant the content is to their lives." You would then select specific data excerpts that help explain what this finding means.[6]

STORIES FROM THE FIELD

Data Analysis in a Study on Conceptual Math Teaching

The assistant superintendent of instruction (Miguel) and three district-level math coaches (Janice, Stephen, and Marie) in a suburban school district recently restructured professional development programming for the district's math teachers to focus on conceptual teaching. The coaches introduced conceptual teaching and explored strategies for how to incorporate it in lessons during two day-long professional development sessions. During the sessions, the math teachers seemed to enjoy discussing conceptual teaching and brainstorming how they could teach concepts in their classrooms differently. In subsequent weeks, the math coaches visited teachers' classrooms throughout the district and reconvened as a group to discuss their observations. The three coaches met with Miguel and noted that they saw little evidence of conceptual teaching in their observations. Thus, they decided to further investigate this issue.

In addition to the three district coaches and the superintendent, the applied research team consisted of two school-based math coaches and two math teachers (one from fourth grade and one from fifth grade), for a total of eight people. The team decided to narrow its focus to grades 4 and 5, as the team believed that upper elementary school offers many opportunities for conceptual teaching. The applied research team developed the following research questions: What are the primary teaching beliefs and practices for fourth- and fifth-grade math teachers in the Smithville School District? What professional development supports, if any, would teachers find beneficial to implement conceptual teaching practices?

To answer these questions, the team reviewed the fourth- and fifth-grade math curricula, conducted twenty observations of the same grades' math classes (divided across eight people so that each member did two or three observations), and conducted five focus groups with fourth- and fifth-grade math teachers. The team members developed a plan for how they would store, record, and organize all the data they collected. All the data were stored on a secure district portal, similar to Dropbox, that was accessed via a school district email and password. All the files were labeled with the date, school, grade level, and pseudonyms of participants. Any identifying information was removed from the data (by an administrative assistant working with the team) before it was uploaded to the portal. The focus groups were audio-recorded, and the superintendent paid to have the recordings professionally transcribed. The team also used an observational fieldnote guide that focused on teachers' explanations of concepts, the questions that teachers and students asked, the responses to those questions, and the prompts for structured activities.

After reviewing the curricula, each team member filled in a data summary form that stated what was and was not included in the various curricular components. The members also noted that the curricula already contained examples of conceptual teaching concepts and strategies, such as the use of real-world examples to guide instruction. The members explained that teachers could therefore incorporate into their lesson plans these strategies that were already in the curricula. All the team members wrote a formative analysis memo after conducting two focus groups. After discussing these memos in a team meeting, they made a few revisions to their focus group instrument and documented potential concepts that the team would use to code their data. After conducting all the observations, each team member wrote a data summary form of what they had learned from the observations. In a whole-team meeting, they then presented their observational learning and shared excerpts from their fieldnotes. Stephen, one of the district coaches, took notes during this meeting and made sure to upload these to the portal where all the meeting notes were kept. For the next team meeting, everyone planned to review the previous meeting's notes, the data summary forms, and the formative analysis memos to prepare for summative analysis.

Before beginning summative data analysis, the researchers developed a set of fifteen codes that they would use when reading their data. These codes included primarily deductive concepts that came from the literature and the coaches' past experiences. Among these codes were *"plug and chug methods," potential for real-world application, differentiated questioning, teaching in a different way than how one learned, one-on-one coaching sessions, peer mentoring,* and *co-planning time.* They did not need to spend a long time defining these codes, as they were all familiar with the math curricula in the school and district, but they still developed brief definitions of these codes so that team members could refer to the definitions while they were coding. The team also decided to remain open to other inductive codes that emerged from the data. The team divided the data, which consisted of five focus groups, twenty observations, and data summary forms for the curricula (preexisting data), among the eight members. Each team member read his or her assigned data and labeled them according to the established codes. The team allocated two weeks for everyone to read and code the data, and then it uploaded the coded data to the shared portal.

At the end of those two weeks, the team members organized their coded data. To facilitate this organizational process, the team members sorted their coded data into separate Word documents for each code. Janice took the lead in combining all the documents for each code and then uploaded them to the shared portal. Thus, there were sixteen files (fifteen for the predetermined codes and one for the additional codes team members developed).

In preparation for the next team meeting, everyone was asked to review the coded data and write a short summative analysis about the themes and other ideas gleaned from the data. To begin this next meeting, each team member spent about five minutes describing what they had written about in the summative analysis memo. Janice took notes about what everyone shared on the white board, and the team spent the rest of the meeting looking at themes supported by data excerpts and deciding which codes could be deleted or combined. The team members decided that everyone should write another short memo reflecting on what they had discussed in this meeting and share it with all team members before the next meeting. In this memo, some of the primary themes that the team noticed were *disconnect between current and former approaches to math teaching, holistic approaches to professional development, significant changes in how math is taught,* and *frustration with the disconnectedness of professional development sessions.*

You might notice that these themes differ from the initial codes that the team developed, but they also reflect how some codes evolved. For example, the team refined and combined some of the initial codes, such as *teaching in a different way than how one learned*, to develop another theme that the group noticed: *disconnect between current and former approaches to math teaching.* This theme was related not only to how teachers learned math but also to how they first learned to teach math.

After spending time discussing the themes, data excerpts, and what they were learning from their data in relation to their research questions and local setting, the team developed two primary findings. First, there is a gap in what teachers describe as best practices for teaching math and what these teachers do when teaching math. A majority of the teachers said that the way they learned math and the way they are being asked to teach it are vastly different. They understand the benefits of the newer approaches, such as conceptual teaching, but they primarily implement more *plug and chug* and rote learning methods, which is also how many teachers first learned how to teach math. Second, teachers expressed that ongoing professional development opportunities (instead of onetime ones) that incorporate mentoring, coaching, and additional time for co-planning lessons would better help them implement new teaching practices such as conceptual teaching. Regarding the gap discussed in the first finding, the teachers believed that their current professional development opportunities were isolated strategies instead of a more holistic, ongoing approach to shift their teaching philosophy and practices.

In chapter 7, we discuss how this team presented these findings to different audiences and how they developed concrete action plans.

PRACTICES TO START

To help your team get started analyzing data, we recommend two practices in addition to the ones we discuss in the chapter (e.g., data summary forms, memos, and data displays). These practices include creating a data analysis plan and engaging in collaborative data analysis.

PRACTICE 16: *Data Analysis Plan*

Brainstorming as a team about all the tasks related to data analysis is one way to develop a data analysis plan and timeline. We recommend being as detailed as possible, setting a completion date for each task, and indicating the person or persons responsible for completing the task. Resource P presents an example of one data analysis plan that is based on our sample process for analyzing data. The following process, which is just one potential way to go about analyzing data, includes numerous tasks. The list also represents a summary of all the steps discussed in this chapter.

- Compose formative analysis memos and data summary forms during data collection.
- Once all your data are collected, develop a data analysis plan and timeline.

- Develop codes, including brief definitions, and use them to label the data.
- Have a meeting to see how people are coding, what questions they have, and so forth.
- Organize the coded data.
- Read and discuss the coded data, the formative data analysis memos, and the data summary forms.
- Compose a summative analysis memo about the themes and other information you gathered from reading and discussing the coded data. Include excerpts of the data that are evidence of these themes.
- Discuss these summative memos in a whole-team meeting focused on coming up with primary findings related to your research questions.
- Think about the story of your data. What are you learning from the data, and how can you best represent that to others?

PRACTICE 17: *Collaborative Data Analysis Workshops*

Collaboratively analyzing data helps teams generate rigorous and useful findings. There are many ways to engage in collaborative data analysis, and we present an overview of one collaborative workshop for your team to consider and modify as needed. A workshop of this type can be repeated multiple times during data analysis, and we recommend repeating the workshop when possible.

This workshop will take approximately one hour, and of that hour, try to allocate forty minutes for smaller-group discussions. Divide your applied research team into groups of two or three people. Each group should review a different set of data. The team must determine in advance which data will be included. For example, you may choose to review excerpts of transcripts or fieldnotes, coded data, preexisting data, data summary forms, or some combination of these types of data. The data you examine may depend on the phase of analysis (i.e., formative or summative analysis).

In addition to determining which data will be included, the team should also decide on the focus of the small-group discussions. For example, the group could discuss the data in relation to the research questions, what stands out, or potential codes. Or the group could compare how all the groups code data, develop themes from the coded data, look for alternate explanations, or develop data displays or conceptual maps.

During the forty minutes allotted for small-group analysis, each person should begin by individually reading the data and jotting down a few notes related to the focus of the workshop. After that time, the small groups will compare their impressions and collaboratively think through the data. Groups could collaboratively develop conceptual maps or other visuals during this time as well. After the small-group discussions, each group will report to the larger group what it has learned (with notetakers assigned), and the team will decide on the next steps.

CHAPTER SUMMARY

This chapter introduced data analysis and detailed how teams can make sense of their data throughout a study and after all the data are collected. The process for analyzing data in applied research involves (1) recording and organizing data; (2) formative data analysis, which includes writing memos and creating data summary forms; and (3) summative analysis of the entire data set by reading and coding data, composing summative analysis memos, and analyzing all the coded data. We shared multiple tips, suggested effective and generative memos, and gave examples of analytical processes to illustrate what analysis of applied research can look like. The example of a team investigating math instruction revealed how one applied research team approached analysis. Finally, the chapter included two practices to help your team analyze data: a detailed data analysis plan and collaborative analysis processes.

SEVEN

Disseminating Findings, Sustaining Action, and Professional Development

THIS CHAPTER FOCUSES on one central question: What do we do with our research? To address this question, we revisit the goals of applied research (and this book): to generate local, sustainable change that is informed by local circumstances. We then detail ways to disseminate your research and to plan for action. To give a concrete example, we describe how a school principal, Kaleb, and his applied research team developed a dissemination plan, presented their findings, convened a task force, and developed a plan for action. We also articulate different ways to structure your reports and presentations, to invite feedback, and to engage and address (and even leverage) dissent and resistance. We conclude by describing how the action from applied research creates opportunities for professional development. Consequently, the practices we suggest at the end of this chapter describe how you can provide ongoing professional development opportunities in connection with your applied research.

Throughout this chapter, we address the following questions:

- What are the best formats for presenting your research findings?

- How can you disseminate your research and act on it?
- How do you create opportunities to receive and incorporate feedback on the research and potential action steps?
- What kinds of professional development opportunities does engagement with, and dissemination of, applied research create?
- How can you ensure the sustainability of your research findings?

FOSTERING CHANGE

Applied research is a way for educational leaders to examine problems or other issues in their practice-based settings. For this reason, a primary goal of applied research is to support local change. The specific goals of your applied research projects will vary. The examples we have presented throughout this book demonstrate the range of goals that educational leaders have for this research. These goals included understanding why test scores were not improving, learning about districtwide approaches to school discipline, examining and creating useful links between theory and practice, and improving the implementation of district initiatives. In all these examples, the goals were to develop an evidence-based approach to examine these topics in locally informed ways and then to develop action plans to help address these issues. In addition to these topic-related goals, additional goals of this research are related to individual and institutional professional development. All these aspects are directly and indirectly related to institutional change. To help bring about this change, we recommend (1) developing a realistic and strategic dissemination plan, (2) presenting data and findings in engaging and accessible ways, and (3) planning and acting according to the research findings.

Developing a Dissemination Plan

Once you have developed key findings from your applied research study, you will want to share this knowledge with a variety of stakeholders to foster change. The way you share your findings will depend on your audiences and the goals of your applied research. As you and your team consider how to disseminate your research findings, we recommend that you consider the following questions:

- Who should we share this work with, and how and when will we do it?
- What are the primary findings that we would like to communicate?
- How can we best invite useful feedback from a range of stakeholders?
- How can we proactively address any anticipated concerns of a range of stakeholders?
- How will we address any potential constraints to disseminating our work?

To describe the processes of disseminating research findings, we revisit an example from chapter 1. Superintendent Eleanor and the ten principals she worked with were studying the purpose of school disciplinary practices at the ten schools in the district. They were also examining how seventh-grade students, teachers, and parents understood these practices. In addition to the research team of Eleanor and the ten principals, each principal had a school-based research team addressing these issues. Because the principals expressed to their teachers that the school disciplinary practices would change as a result of the research, the teachers were especially excited to be a part of the research teams, and they engaged in the entire process with focus and vigor.

In this example, there are clearly multiple goals and purposes going on, including to understand collectively (as a district) and individually (as a school) the practices of school discipline. In addition to gaining a better understanding of the issue from various perspectives, an ultimate goal was to change school and district discipline practices as a result of the insight gained. In the next section, we demonstrate how one school disseminated the results of its applied research.

STORIES FROM THE FIELD

Sharing Knowledge with a Diverse Community

Kaleb, a school principal on Eleanor's district research team, and his own school-based research team developed a plan to present their findings to all the relevant stakeholders. To develop this plan, the team brainstormed who these stakeholders were and how they could best share information with these groups. They determined that their primary stakeholders included (1) the entire faculty and staff of the school; (2) the superintendent, Eleanor, and the other principals in the district; (3) the seventh-grade students, and (4) the parents and guardians of seventh-grade students. Keeping these audiences in mind, the research team developed a two-page executive summary containing five elements:

- their research questions
- an overview of the school context
- three primary findings, along with short illustrative quotes from participants for each finding
- any questions remaining
- potential ideas for action

Kaleb and the research team then shared this executive summary with Eleanor, their fellow principals, and a small group of school faculty members to get feedback. Using this feedback, Kaleb and his team developed a presentation to share their research and findings with the entire school faculty and staff. A goal of this presentation was to share what they had learned and to receive feedback, including input from the rest of the school personnel about action steps that the team could take. The team members also planned to receive input from students and parents, but they wanted to first make sure that the faculty and staff were aware of the findings before the data were presented to other stakeholders.

After presenting to the faculty and staff and receiving their input about the research and potential action plans, the researchers modified their presentation for a student audience. They shortened the presentation, put it in language tailored to seventh-grade students, and included hands-on activities to engage the children with the findings and to solicit suggestions for future action. These activities included small-group conversations for students to discuss their thoughts about the research findings, a silent gallery walk in which students could give personal reactions to potential action steps, and a whole-group discussion on how to move forward. The team also set up a box in which the students could place any comments they did not want to share during the group sessions. The team sent students home with a one-page flyer about the research for them to share with their parents or guardians. This flyer included a link where families could directly respond to the research team with their input. An electronic version of the flyer and link were also emailed directly to the students' homes.

Thus, the dissemination plan and timeline involved careful consideration of how, when, with whom, and in what order the team would share its findings and invite feedback. And as a result, the team received valuable feedback from important stakeholders.

Knowing Your Audiences

As we have discussed, the decisions about what format to present the research depend on the audiences and goals of the study. Kaleb and his team wrote an executive summary, developed presentations, and created an inviting and engaging flyer. As superintendent, Eleanor had different audiences for her research, and one goal was to inform the district about the practices and to present the findings to practitioners and scholars. In addition to presenting to her colleagues, Eleanor and a few principals presented the research at an academic conference. Of course, the presentation guidelines for this type of conference were considerably different from those for the presentation to district officials. At the academic conference, for example, the presentation was limited to fifteen minutes, with five minutes for questions.

In contrast, Kaleb's presentation to the entire faculty and staff lasted more than an hour, and the presentation was structured to be engaging and solicit feedback. For another audience, the applied research team began its presentation to the entire school with a vignette that illustrated one of the key findings, which is that students experience disciplinary-oriented microaggressions that can lead to racial inequity in the enforcement of school rules. To help the faculty and staff understand this issue from a range of students' perspectives, the team presented a vignette of Kareem, a seventh-grade biracial male student, to illustrate the different kinds of interactions that a student may experience in one day. The goal was to show how many of these interactions are related to racial identity and what happens when schools fail to approach discipline from a holistic, equity-oriented, and identity-informed perspective.

The vignette describes how during first period, Kareem is asked in a disparaging way to "quiet down" by a white male teacher during group work. Kareem tells the teacher that everyone else is talking, and the teacher responds by saying that Kareem is talking louder than the other students are. One of Kareem's friends, a white girl, defends Kareem, noting how unfair the teacher was. She says that she was actually talking the loudest in their group. Kareem feels that he is being unfairly targeted because everyone in the class is talking, and his friends confirm that he is not being louder than other students. Kareem feels that he has been disrespected by this teacher.

In second period, Kareem has finished his assignment early and with all the correct answers; he receives a hall pass to go to the water fountain. A white male security guard hollers at Kareem to get back to class without knowing (or checking to see) that Kareem had permission to be at the water fountain.

In third period, Kareem is publicly embarrassed by a black female teacher for not knowing the answer right away in math class. She says, "Come on, Kareem. You of all people should know this." Kareem does not respond, but later he shared with the researchers his feelings of being singled out, embarrassed, and angry.

During lunch, a staff member asks Kareem to pick up trash from under the table even though he is sitting with six peers. Kareem responds that he did not throw trash on the floor, and the staff member, a black woman, tells him to stop speaking back to her. He picks up the trash, but he is quite angry and feels constantly criticized and held to a different standard than what his majority white peers are held to.

Then, in fifth period, Kareem, along with a group of other students, is given a detention for not having his homework completed. Kareem hollers, "This is so unfair! Why am I getting a detention? I didn't understand the homework, it's my first time not finishing an assignment all year, and I emailed the teacher last night." The teacher, a white woman, tells Kareem that he has a bad attitude and tells him to be quiet. Exasperated, Kareem yells, "I am so sick of this school, it's so unfair!" and walks out of the classroom. The teacher then notifies the office, and the security guard is sent to find him.

The team members used the structure of the vignette to begin the presentation as a reference point. They hoped the faculty and staff could start thinking about the racial inequity of Kareem's experience with school discipline and see how these disciplinary encounters affected the students both individually and collectively. To help faculty and staff understand how these kinds of situations happen, the team presented the frame of racial microaggressions. As discussed in chapter 2, racial microaggressions are common, often brief verbal, behavioral, or environmental indignities, either intentional or unintentional, that routinely communicate racial slights and greater insults toward people of color.[1] This concept proved useful in helping people to understand how daily school life affects people such as Kareem and any other person from a non-dominant group.

Using Kareem's experiences, the team showed how some of his interactions were microaggressions. The team members chose his interaction with the security guard to facilitate a conversation about implicit bias. Would the guard have stopped a white student in the same way? Why or why not? Then they extended this definition to look across the gamut of actions the adults in the building took toward Kareem that day and to consider the overall student experience and the resulting school environment. This approach generated a powerful all-group conversation about how deficit orientations, and the implicit biases they are built on, played out in each person's disciplinary approach as well as in the collective. People saw Kareem's experiences in new ways, and many admitted that the situation of microaggressions was worse than anyone had realized. Furthermore, the faculty decided to request a series of professional development sessions focused on implicit bias as it relates to discipline and classroom management.

The previous example comes from a school we worked with a few years ago. But regardless of the format, topic, and audience, we recommend that you think about how you will structure your findings, who the audiences are, how the data will be incorporated, how you will include sufficient contextual information and participant voices, and if and how potential action steps will be presented. The remainder of this section addresses these components.

Structure, Format, and Audience
Research can be presented in many ways, including printed reports, in-person presentations, and even a short video, a podcast, or a series of tweets with links. The most effective format depends on the intended audience and potential constraints such as time and money. Regardless of the format, we recommend that the research be presented clearly and be accessible to your audience. To help you get started, we have included some possibilities to consider when you begin sharing your research. However, your reports or presentations may be different from these suggestions, depending on the audiences, your goals, the context, and the stakeholders' expectations.

For a report or presentation, you can prepare an introduction that describes the topic you studied, explains why it is important, states the research questions, and provides relevant contextual information. As you are describing the importance of the topic, you may also briefly integrate the literature that you reviewed in the introduction or during the main part of the presentation. Anticipating your audience in terms of what will resonate or turn people off is key (and requires proactive team dialogue and planning).

Next, you will give an overview of the research process that your team used to examine this topic. You and your team should transparently describe who conducted the research, why the research was necessary, what methods were used, the data you collected, and how the data were analyzed. For example, Kaleb and his team stated in their executive summary that they interviewed four seventh-grade teachers; conducted three focus groups, each consisting of six seventh-grade students; sent out an open-ended survey to seventh-grade students and their parents; and analyzed a total of thirty student and twenty parent survey responses. The researchers also noted that they reviewed school discipline statistics for the past five years for the seventh grade and analyzed officially documented school policies. Finally, Kaleb and his team described how they composed data contact forms after each interview and focus group, wrote and shared formative analysis memos with each other, and analyzed their data using a thematic approach. Depending on the structure of your report or presentation, the description of your research methods may be more or less detailed. Since Kaleb was writing a two-page executive summary, he and his team chose to limit the amount of detail in this section.

Some members of your audience may not be familiar with your research methods. For example, Jennifer, the assistant head of school at Middleberry Independent School, and her research team decided that in light of their audience, which included school faculty, they needed to first devote a presentation to teaching the rest of the faculty about applied research and overviewing the processes the team used. Jennifer's team wanted to preemptively address questions and critiques of their research methods since many of the faculty were unfamiliar with qualitative research. After this presentation, Jennifer and the team felt ready to share their research findings.

After you tell your audience how you collected and analyzed data, you will present your primary findings. As chapter 6 describes, we recommend including approximately three findings. Of course, depending on your research, you may include more or fewer. Each finding represents a broader theme from your data. Thus, as you present your thematic findings, you may consider beginning with an overview of all of your findings and then describing each finding individually. As you individually describe each thematic finding, explain what that theme means and how it is emblematic of your data.

For example, when Kaleb was describing the team's first theme, which included the observation that rules were inconsistently enforced and understood, the team clarified that this theme was present in interviews with teachers, focus groups with seventh-grade students and families, and that a review of the school policies and records also reflected this theme. Your themes might not always be supported by all your data sources. Thus, it becomes important to clearly specify the data that do support your findings. As you explain what a theme or finding means, you will also review the data that support it, such as excerpts or quotes from interviews, focus groups, or observations. You might also summarize quantitative data in a table or highlight what you learned from a review of documents. You can also include visual data displays or other means of representing your data (e.g., figure 6.5).

When incorporating data in write-ups and presentations, you need to keep a few key factors in mind. First, data do not speak for themselves. If you provide a quote, table, document, or chart, you should walk the audience through what the piece of data means and how it relates to the overall findings.

Another important aspect is the participants' privacy. For example, Kaleb interviewed four teachers, and when he presented quotes from these teachers, he did not include any identifying characteristics. As is often the case with applied research studies that take place in an organization, the identity of the participants can easily be deduced. Thus, as discussed in chapter 5, you have to alert people, before they participate in the study, that their anonymity could be inadvertently compromised. Moreover, you and your research team must be sensitive to the participants' privacy wishes and make sure to protect their privacy.

In presenting your data, you may also bring in relevant literature to show how your findings compare with these previous studies. Again, depending on your audience, situating your research in relevant literature may be more or less important. For example, when Eleanor presented her research at an academic conference, she included a discussion of her research in relation to previous research in the field.

The final section of a presentation or report is typically the conclusion and implications. Here, you are letting your audience know why this research is important and what can be learned from it. The implications for this research are likely to be the development of an action plan. Again, depending on the audience, this part of your report or presentation might be an opportunity to solicit feedback about potential action steps and the constraints on such steps. After presenting your findings to multiple groups of stakeholders and receiving feedback from them, the next step is often the development of an action plan, a step we discuss in the next section.

Planning and Acting

One of the hoped-for results of applied research is actionable change. This change will look different, depending on the goals of the research. For example, the assistant superintendent of instruction, Miguel, and three district-level math coaches in the suburban Smithville School District conducted research about fourth- and fifth-grade math teachers' beliefs and practices and what professional development support would best help teachers implement conceptual teaching practices. The research findings suggested a gap between what teachers describe as "best practices" for teaching math and what these teachers actually do when teaching math. In addition, the research suggests that ongoing, instead of onetime, professional development opportunities that incorporate mentoring, coaching, and additional time for co-planning lessons would better help teachers implement new teaching practices, including conceptual teaching. In light of the findings and feedback from various stakeholders, the research team developed a set of action steps that included structuring additional planning time so that fourth- and fifth-grade math teachers could incorporate conceptual teaching into their preexisting practices. For example, the research showed that teachers in the district regularly used project-based assignments, and since these assignments are a good opportunity to implement additional conceptual teaching practices, one action plan included providing additional collaborative planning time each week for teachers to incorporate conceptual teaching into those project-based assignments.

In addition to this planning time, a district math coach met with fourth- and fifth-grade teachers twice a month to provide ongoing support for conceptual teaching and to observe teachers and follow up on their daily practices. One math specialist worked with a team of teachers at each school, and this team collaboratively developed goals related to conceptual teaching practices and other goals that the teachers had identified. As a part of the action plan, members of the research team followed up with all the district coaches after six months to assess the progress being made with these action steps.

Again, action steps and plans will look differently, depending on multiple factors. Examples of action can also be onetime changes, such as revising curricula or grading guidelines for faculty. Actions can also be a series of ongoing events, including ongoing professional development or a year-long orientation program for freshman students to focus on issues of equity. Sometimes, the action might be the implementation of additional research needed to help the team decide on the most sustainable action steps. Regardless of where your team is in the process, we recommend making a plan that includes (1) the proposed action steps, (2) the potential barriers to those steps, (3) the stakeholders needed to implement the steps, (4) a reasonable timeline for implementation, and (5) a reflection and follow-up period in which the team checks in to see how and if action steps are working.

Anticipating Potential Barriers

As summarized above, part of the action plan we recommend is the anticipation of potential barriers or other constraints to the action steps. As discussed throughout the book, you and your applied research team must think about and proactively address organizational change. You need to pay close attention to contextual factors that make up your organizational culture and understand how the research aligns or diverges from this culture. For example, as you learn more about your organization's culture, you can better anticipate potential resistance to your research and who may resist your findings and recommended action. Being aware of how individuals may be hesitant to change and creating opportunities for these individuals to be heard and engaged often increases the success of potential action. Another way to troubleshoot the negative responses is to connect the research with organizational mission and vision statements so that the research is related to the stated goals of the institution. In addition, the collaborative nature of this work, which can sometimes make the process more complex, also helps validate the research when many stakeholders and well-respected individuals are a part of the research.

Including Stakeholders

To illustrate planning for action, we continue our discussion of Kaleb and his research team. After sharing their research with multiple stakeholders and hearing the stakeholders' feedback on the findings and potential action steps, the team formed a school discipline task force led by Kaleb. He decided to lead this task force because he wanted to assure the participants that he was serious about implementing change. The task force convened toward the end of the school year, and the individuals who volunteered to take part decided to work over the summer so that they could develop and implement a plan beginning the following school year.

One of the team's primary findings was the inconsistent enforcement of the discipline rules for the seventh grade and the variable interpretation of these rules by multiple stakeholders, including students, teachers, parents, and guardians. Part of this finding included racial disparities in the enforcement of rules, as demonstrated by the experiences of students like Kareem. As a consequence, a majority of seventh-grade students, teachers, and their parents and guardians felt frustration, confusion, and disappointment regarding the discipline system. Thus, the goal of the newly formed task force was to begin to develop a consensus on what the current policies and rules regarding student conduct in the seventh grade meant. The task force was to study how these rules should be revised and to develop guidelines for how they should be interpreted. Finally, the group was charged with designing a way for students and staff to better communicate with each other when disputes about enforcement (or lack thereof) of the code of conduct arose.

Besides Kaleb, the task force included two staff members from the research team at his school, two seventh-grade students, and one seventh-grade parent. As the task force worked together, the members held several town hall meetings in which they presented their current work and invited feedback from students, teachers, and parents. The task force also met with Kaleb's research team to develop a detailed action plan and timeline. Kaleb and other members of the research team wanted to use this experience with the seventh grade to inform other practices and norms in the rest of their school, so they also put additional data collection to this timeline. In addition, the applied research team mapped out how they could address other aspects of their findings, including teachers' perceptions of student behavior. Kaleb and the team decided that they would present a series of collaborative workshops to the faculty during professional development meetings. Thus, the action plan the team developed was a year-long plan to address their findings and involved multiple stakeholders and different strategies for generating change, including implementing the recommendations of the task force.

In addition to developing the task force, the faculty came up with an additional action step after hearing the research team's presentation. The faculty believed that they needed help in developing an awareness of how rules are enforced differently according to students' racial identities. They wanted to learn how to blame neither students of color nor individual teachers but to help the adults think about their own racial bias and what they are communicating to the black male students in the class. Thus, the faculty decided to develop a partner system in which each member of the faculty was given a partner, and the partners would take turns observing each other's class with the lens of racial disparity, microaggressions, and racial stress. Thus, in this environment, each teacher could unpack what was going on in the classroom and the potential reasons behind anyone's actions.

Setting a Timeline for Reflection and Follow-Up

Finally, an additional part of this plan helped generate sustainable change. The team members from Kaleb's school included deliberate, carefully timed check-ins in their action plan so that they could assess their steps and collect additional data as needed throughout the school year and during professional development sessions. By sharing their research, Kaleb and his team learned that teachers and staff members throughout the school, not just in seventh grade, often misinterpreted student behavior in similar ways. Thus, Kaleb included multiple collaborative professional development sessions that different stakeholders in the school community led to help teachers and staff members think about different interpretations of student behavior.

As a way to ensure the sustainability of your research findings and actions, it can be helpful to view professional development as an ongoing process. Kaleb and his team approached their professional development sessions in this way, by not considering their action steps as onetime sessions or as checkboxes to be completed. Instead, they looked at their research as an ongoing process of inquiry and development. In this regard, the acts of engaging in applied research constitute examples of ongoing professional development opportunities.

PRACTICES TO START

We have presented many practical applications throughout this chapter, including the suggestion to develop a thorough dissemination plan and a detailed plan for action. In addition to those ideas, we offer suggestions for building ongoing professional development on the findings of your applied research and for the systematic reflection on the research and action.

PRACTICE 18: *Topical Professional Development Based on Applied Research*

To help ensure sustainable change in your school or district, you can provide professional development offerings that are directly connected to the applied research findings. For example, the district officials studying how to improve conceptual teaching in math implemented professional development sessions for teachers, basing the sessions on findings about the gaps in teachers' conceptual teaching practices.

Professional development sessions based on research findings need not be in the form of an action step. They can be a part of the life cycle of your research as you and your team learn new ideas. For example, Jennifer gave a presentation on applied research to the entire faculty at Middleberry Independent School. After her presentation, many people were interested in conducting this type of research themselves, and others were interested in being involved in a future applied research project. Thus, as you are conducting your research, many professional development opportunities for yourself and your colleagues may arise, and we hope that you use these opportunities to further the professional development of your organization.

For example, if you were the leader of the applied research team that was addressing the findings about Kareem, you could work with your team to design peer-level professional development offerings about racial inequity, microaggressions, and misinterpreting student behavior. *Peer-level* means that leaders would engage in professional development with peer-level leaders—teachers with teachers, staff with staff, and so on. This kind of grouping, in our experience, can enable participants to share their experiences with each other in more relatable ways and to feel less self-conscious, because they are not sharing questions and struggles across school or district hierarchies.

PRACTICE 19: *Ongoing Systematic Reflection on Research and Action*

To engage in applied research for sustainable change and ongoing professional development, we encourage you and the members of your applied research team to develop an ongoing practice of systematically reflecting on your research and action. The process of reflection on research and action, which is also referred to as *praxis*, involves specific practices to ensure that you individually and collaboratively assess and reassess your research and the actions that have resulted from it. For example, after your team has implemented an action that resulted from your applied research project, we recommend that members of the team reflect on the effectiveness of this action. This reflection can be written in a memo or can include other kinds of testimonials and quotes from participants, whose opinions you gather and then share with other members of the applied research team. We culminate this book with this concept of praxis since it weds reflection with action, and we argue that applied research is the connective tissue that enables relevant, responsive praxis that is both individual and collective.

Praxis can take many forms, including writing memos and brief reports that examine the impact of the action steps and sharing these reflections with multiple stakeholders and listening to their feedback. Praxis may also involve collecting and analyzing additional data to better understand how the action steps are being implemented. Depending on what you learn, you may also decide to start a new applied research project. At the heart of these processes of reflection on research and action is the necessity of engaging in dialogue with others to help inform your research and action.

The overarching point here is that when you are developing and implementing action, you need to consider how to continue to reflect and collect data about what is going on, how your actions are affecting people in the setting, and what inspired the research in the first place. It can be useful to recruit additional stakeholders to help with praxis, but it can also be the job of those on the applied research team, since they are already involved and can track the progress as a community of practice over time.

CHAPTER SUMMARY

A goal of this chapter is to help you determine how to disseminate your research—to whom, in what format, and for what purpose—and then to develop a concrete plan for action based on your research. We discussed several important considerations to guide your decision-making and detailed examples of what these processes can look like. We concluded this chapter by highlighting the goals of applied research in fostering sustainable change as well as how action is linked to professional development. In the next chapter, we argue that applied research processes, such as developing questions, collaborating with stakeholders, and collecting data, are themselves professional development opportunities for individuals and institutions.

CONCLUSION

Applied Research and Sustainable Organizational Change

APPLIED RESEARCH HAS the power to transform educational organizations. In addition to the organizational changes driven by this kind of local site-focused research, applied research also presents transformative opportunities for you as a leader, for all the members of your research team, and, ultimately, for the rest of your educational community.

Applied educational research is an approach to continuous improvement and professional development. Now, arguably more than ever, there is an increasing need for local knowledge creation through site-based research. It is our hope that this book will help you, your colleagues, and your employees cultivate the kinds of reflective processes, research skills, and inquiry dispositions that will ultimately make education better and more equitable for all students.

Applied research presents many opportunities for professional development. In addition to creating opportunities for professional development as potential action steps, applied research opens numerous pathways to personal professional development for you and members of the applied research team.

Some of these pathways focus on the leadership mindsets and skills necessary for this type of research. Among these attitudes and skills are the willingness to (1) situate yourself as a learner, (2) reconsider data and research, (3) view collaboration as integral to professional excellence and development, and (4) challenge the status quo of your organization. By engaging in applied research processes, you continue to reinforce these aspects of practice and support yourself and your colleagues in cultivating them. For example, the success of applied research projects often depends on how you, the leader, convey what the research will be used for and demonstrate how you are engaged in the process yourself as a learner. By expanding what counts as data and using applied research to better understand topics, you are also modeling this process of inquiry to your staff and colleagues. Thus, as we have described throughout the book, collaboration is central to the success of applied research projects and to sustaining change. By engaging in this research with the goal of learning through leadership and collaboration, you are challenging the status quo of education and educational systems (with a focus on your own), modeling that for others, and presenting different possibilities for education.

In figure 8.1, we detail some of the potential professional development opportunities that the applied research process can generate. We have heard from many educational leaders that the mere practice of applied research generates valuable learning in and of itself. For example, you and the members of your team learn how to think carefully about research questions; listen to different stakeholders to understand a diversity of viewpoints; develop team goals and norms; cultivate research, writing, and communication skills; examine theories and professional practices; and foster analytical and critical thinking skills. These are just some of some of the many professional development opportunities that engaging in applied research can offer.

As you and your research team cultivate the skills, mindsets, and knowledge needed for conducting applied research, you can also consider providing your colleagues and educators with the skills to better assess their own practices. Thus, as an educational leader, you can, for example, include as many of your colleagues and staff as possible in this type of inquiry. You can also

Applied Research and Sustainable Organizational Change 181

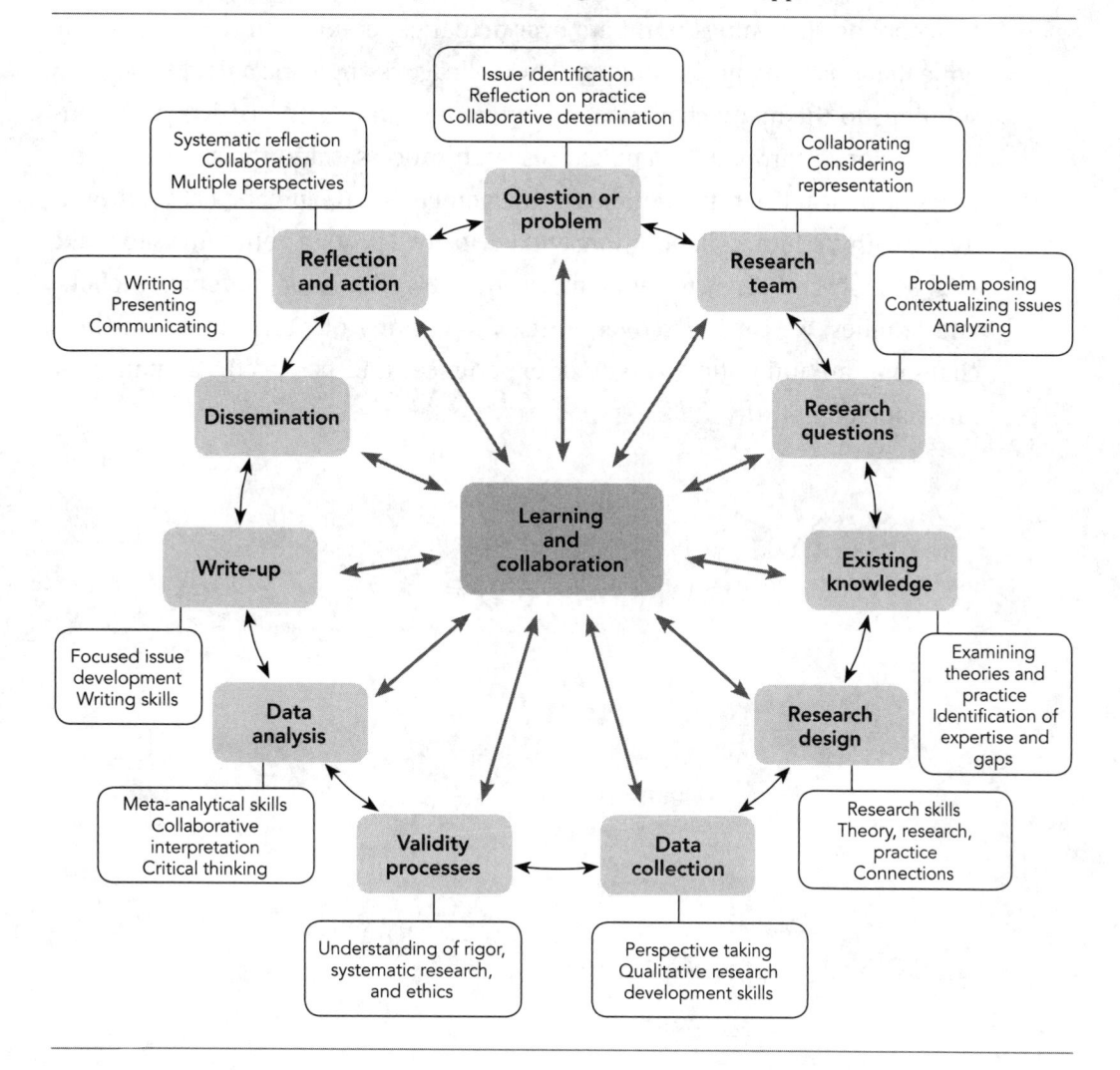

FIGURE 8.1 Professional development offerings connected to applied research

encourage the people around you to situate themselves as learners engaged in a process of research, reflection, and action.

A learner stance and an appreciation of locally generated knowledge are crucial in this current education and policy climate in the United States. Applied research for sustainable change presents opportunities to help you, as an educational leader, resist the often generic and dehumanizing approach to schooling that values numbers over actual experiences. In this regard, we hope that this book helps you and your colleagues apply local data to develop solutions to the many challenges facing your schools and districts. Solutions are developed through the applied research processes and the skills and attitudes of critical listening, authentic engagement, an open perspective, humility, empathy, ethics, collaboration, and curiosity. Through your efforts to make your schools and districts better, more equitable places for students, teachers, and families, we can collectively resist the tyranny of numbers and instead champion an authentic diversity of experiences and perspectives in all their range and complexity.

APPENDIX

List of Practices to Get Started

Chapter 1
1. Situating Yourself as a Learner
2. Reconsidering Qualitative Research and Data
3. Fostering Collaboration as Integral to Professional Excellence
4. Challenging the Status Quo

Chapter 2
5. Focus Walks
6. Flash Focus Groups (Small-Group Discussions)

Chapter 3
7. Topic-Exploration Memo
8. Existing-Knowledge Memo
9. Applied Research Design Template

Chapter 4
10. Assessing Biases and Blind Spots
11. Introducing and Cocreating Brave Spaces

Chapter 5
12. Data Collection Plan and Timeline
13. Aligning Data Collection Methods with Research Questions
14. Reflexive Data Collection Through Mini Memos
15. Refining Research Instruments

Chapter 6
16. Data Analysis Plan
17. Collaborative Data Analysis Workshops

Chapter 7
18. Topical Professional Development Based on Applied Research
19. Ongoing Systematic Reflection on Research and Action

RESOURCES

RESOURCE A:
Additional Readings on Brave Spaces[1]

Brian Arao and Kristi Clemens, "From Safe Spaces to Brave Spaces: A New Way to Frame Dialogue Around Diversity and Social Justice." in *The Art of Effective Facilitation: Reflections from Social Justice Educators*, edited by Lisa M. Landreman, 135–150. Sterling, VA: Stylus Publishing, 2013.

    We highly recommend reading this chapter with your team. It clearly differentiates between safe and brave spaces, showing the importance of brave spaces that are responsive to multiple conceptions of safety and risk-taking. Arao and Clemens, whose work we have referenced several times in our discussion of brave spaces, provide a solid rationale for why working toward safe spaces can be problematic, given that it tends to favor white, middle-class, male-dominant norms and ways of communicating. This chapter also helps the reader think about group norms, what the authors refer to as "ground rules" for this concept. They provide concrete strategies for developing these ground rules and pushing team members to think about their decisions.

Sherry K. Watt, "The Practice of Freedom: Leading Through Controversy." In *Developing Culturally Relevant Leadership Learning*, edited by Kathy L. Guthrie, Tamara Bertrand Jones, and Laura Osteen, 35–46. San Francisco: Jossey Bass, 2016.

    In this source, which is a useful framework for leaders and team members, Sherry Watt argues that engaging in dialogue about controversial issues develops skills in leaders and group members and fosters individual and collective transformation. She proposes a framework she calls "authentic, action-oriented framing for environmental shifts" as a way for leaders to identify the skills necessary for facing difficult issues. Watts recommends a concept similar to reflexivity, suggesting that leaders reflect on their personal experiences and then create "ground rules" for discussing difficult topics.

Lynn Verduzco-Baker, "Modified Brave Spaces: Calling in Brave Instructors." *Sociology of Race and Ethnicity* (April 2018): 1–8.

Lynn Verduzco-Baker focuses on two aspects of brave spaces. The article looks at the differences between "dialogic-based social justice workshops" and more conventional classroom settings, and it offers suggestions for cultivating brave spaces in these same classrooms. The article is more geared toward classroom-based instructors, but the suggestions are equally relevant for school leaders hoping to create brave spaces among their faculty. Verduzco-Baker proposes three steps that instructors can take to create brave spaces in their conventional classrooms. First, instructors should integrate "virtual personal experiences," which consist of essays, blogs, videos, and other sources that depict firsthand experiences of oppression, into their curriculum to lessen the burden on marginalized students. With these virtual experiences, marginalized children don't have to share their own (often painful) narratives to educate their more privileged peers. Second, instructors initiate a process of "calling in" to address problematic statements and questions. Besides modeling this process, instructors explicitly explain why and how students should call each other (and their instructors) in, rather than call them out. Finally, instructors must model appropriate responses to being called in, which include resisting defensiveness and taking responsibility for one's own education.

RESOURCE B:
Topics for Focus Walks

Environment
- What is the general atmosphere in the school or district office? What about the school board or city council meetings?
- What physical features and observable behaviors convey this atmosphere?
- What is the flow and energy like in the hallways, classrooms, offices, and meetings?
- How does the look and feel of the entrance convey the school's or district's priorities? Does it message different things to different people? Why and how?

Physical Space
- What is displayed on the desks, walls, and lockers of a school?
- What is displayed in the district offices or central administration offices?
- Are there common areas, and how and by whom are they utilized?
- Where are people located in the building? How is space is allocated to different people?
- What is the overall feel of the building?

Communication norms
- How do people communicate with one another?
- What kinds of emotion are expressed at various times of the day and in various activities and spaces?
- What kinds of communication are most common or emblematic of the organization's culture?
- What kinds of communication behaviors seem to create tension? Why does this seem to be so?

RESOURCE C:
Flash Focus Group Topics and Questions

Culture
- What would you tell a new hire about the institution, and why?
- What do you like most about working here?
- What three adjectives best describe the organization, and why?
- Who is respected here, and why?
- Who is not respected here, and why not?
- What does respect mean to different people?
- What is the range of cultures and subcultures here? What are the groups and subgroups?
- What are the dynamics within and between various groups in the organization? *Follow-up questions may relate to identity groups, formal roles, and so on.*
- Do you feel that there is ample representation and equity in leadership across faculty, staff, and students? Why or why not?
- How would you describe the emotional climate of the organization?
- What are two or three artifacts of the organization's culture? What do they represent?
- What one thing would you most like to change about this organization?
- What do you think the different stakeholders (e.g., teachers, principals, district officials, students, parents) value, and why?

Mission and vision
- What three words stand out to you about the mission? We recommend giving everyone time to write these down and then share with the small group. After everyone has shared, the group might collectively consider the differences. You should also remind participants that there are no right or wrong answers.
- How are the organization's priorities aligned with the mission? Why or why not?
- How do the practices of the school or district policy reflect the organization's mission?
- Ask different stakeholders (in their respective focus groups) to read the mission and vision statements aloud. Then invite each person, one at a time, to critique them and relate them to their own experiences at the school. During these conversations, ask the rest of the group about what stands out about the topics or ideas that another member brings up.
- Make sure to ask participants to give specific examples of what they are discussing.

Priorities

- What are three institutional priorities? Are these shared across stakeholder groups?
- Are these priorities relevant and useful? Are they are communicated and understood collectively? Are they taken up in the daily functioning of the organization?
- If there are competing priorities, what are they? What systemic issues relate to these priorities? Are there power struggles over priorities?
- What are the formal and informal values of the organization? How are these values enacted (or not enacted)?
- How/are the organization's priorities messaged to/known by each stakeholder group?

Systems and policies

- What formal policies guide the work of the organization?
- What informal policies guide the work?
- What is the relationship between formal and informal policies?
- What is the process for evaluating policies? Who is involved?
- How does the institutional structure mediate new ideas, programs, and collaboration?
- How are internal policy decisions made? Who is involved, and how are the decisions communicated to the faculty, staff, students, parents, board, and so forth?
- What roles and responsibilities (formal and informal) do people play? Are these a part of their job descriptions? Performance appraisals? Are people given incentives to take on these roles? Is there inequity in how these roles and responsibilities are assigned?
- Are there informal roles or responsibilities that people take on that are problematic?
- Do aspects of the physical space constrain activities and other processes (such as collaboration, mentoring, community learning)? How so or how not?
- How much bureaucracy is in your organization? Does bureaucracy, in the form of institutional rules and policies, constrain innovative professional practices? Which ones are affected?

Organizational structures

These questions and topics would probably be discussed in your leadership team meetings and with your applied research team.

- Is there a strategic plan in place, and should there be?
- When was the last strategic planning process? How did that go, and how was it implemented?
- Does your team conduct any sort of organizational self-assessment? If so, and if it was productive and well received, then build on that success. If it was not useful or was even

harmful to the organizational ethos, then clearly indicate how the current effort will depart from that approach.
- Examine all professional development programs and support to determine their effectiveness and role in your overall organization.
- Review your organization's performance appraisal process. How it can be improved with feedback from those appraised?

RESOURCE D:
Applied Research Design Template

Research topic and goals • What is the research topic? • Why is this topic important? • What are the primary goals of the research?	
Research questions • What are the guiding research questions for the study? • How do the research questions reflect the goals of the study? • Are the research questions clear?	
Existing knowledge • What do I and the rest of the research team already know about the topic? • What literature and theories will we review to better understand the topic? • What existing documents, data, or other resources will we use?	
Connection to preexisting data, missions, and policies • Does the study stem from, or inform, preexisting data? If so, which data, and how? • Does the study connect to the school or institutional mission? If so, how? • How does the research align with the organizational culture and values?	
Research methods • What data collection methods does our team plan to use? • What permissions (e.g., approval from school or district research board, consent forms) are needed to collect data? • How will the data be recorded? For example, will interviews be audio-recorded and transcribed? • How will these methods be sequenced? • How will the data be stored and organized? • How will we analyze the data early on to inform the later parts of our study?	

Participants • Who will be included as participants in the study? • Why will we choose these people? Why not others? • Do we have adequate representation of intersectional identities and groups? • How will our team protect the participants' privacy?	
Validity • How will the research design promote validity? • How will our research team ensure that our findings are as accurate as possible? • How can we challenge interpretations throughout the research?	
Time and other resources • How will this study be best accomplished? • What resources, including time, are needed to ensure its success? • How can I make myself and the team accountable for this research? • How can the research be incorporated into preexisting structures (e.g., prep time, professional development)?	
Action plans • Where does our research team see the potential for action? • Who are the different audiences for the research? • What potential challenges do we anticipate with respect to taking action?	
Timeline • What is the timeline for conducting the research? • When will data collection be complete? • Have we built in enough time to refine our methods and to check in with participants? • What is the timeline for data analysis? For presenting our findings? For developing action plans?	

RESOURCE E:
Questions to Guide Personal and Group Discussion of Biases and Blind Spots

Passion-related biases and blind spots
- What am I passionate about? What guides this passion?
- What are my educational priorities? Why these and not others?
- How does this passion or priority play out in my practice as an educator?
- How might this passion or priority lead to biases? Which biases?
- What could be the result of these biases?
- How might this passion or priority lead to blind spots in my practice as an educator?
- What are possible implications of these blind spots?

Prejudice-related biases and blind spots
- What prejudices do I have about specific social identity groups? Professional groups? Social classes? What evidence do I have that challenges these prejudices?
- How could the school/district/organization be a more inclusive and resonant place for all people?
- Who is often left out when I think of the student body? The faculty? Why?
- What are my feelings about youth culture today? About the role of technology in students' lives? About their values and beliefs?
- Am I biased toward students, teachers, or parents with various mental health issues or learning differences? If so, in what ways?
- What frustrates me about professional discussions about equity? Why?
- Am I aware of how my social identity (i.e., the intersections of race, gender, culture, religion, and other social factors) shapes my thinking? How does it shape how others perceive me? What about how I perceive them?

RESOURCE F:
Example of an Interview Instrument for Teachers, Counselors, and Advisers, First Draft

Date	
Time	
Interviewer	
Notetaker	
Participant name and role	
Location (e.g., classroom, office, coffee shop, over the phone)	
Reviewed and signed consent form	☐ Yes
Consent to be audio-recorded	☐ Yes ☐ No
Opening script (The script does not need to be read verbatim, but it can help guide how you will begin the interview.)	*The goal of this interview is to better understand what you believe ninth-grade students' experiences are with stress and other challenges so that we, as a school, can better support all students. Your responses will be shared with members of the research team, and we will keep your answers confidential. You do not have to answer any question, and we can stop the interview at any time. This interview will take approximately thirty to forty-five minutes. Do you have any questions for me before we begin? Okay, I am now, with your permission, going to turn on the recorder.*

Questions

1. *To begin, can you tell me how long you've been working here and your current role?*
   Potential follow-up question:
   - *Where did you work before you started working here? What was your role there?*

2. *How would you characterize ninth-grade students' school experiences in general?*
   Follow-up questions:
   - *Can you name one of the more positive aspects of their experiences?*
   - *Can you name one of the less positive aspects?*

3. *During your time here, what have you noticed about the challenges that ninth-grade students face?*
   Follow-up questions:
   - *Can you share an example of one of these challenges?*
   - *How do the challenges here compare with ninth-grade students' experiences at previous schools you have worked?*

4. *The ninth-grade students report having high levels of stress. Have you seen that play out in your interactions with these students? If so, how does this stress manifest itself?*

    Follow-up questions:

    - *Please describe one or two examples in which a student demonstrated signs of stress and what that looked like.*
    - *Please share any statements students have shared about stress and other challenges.* (Students' names should not be used.)

5. *How do you support students who are experiencing challenges?*

    Follow-up question:

    - Ask for an example of a time the teacher supported a student and what this looked like.

6. *In your opinion, what are the root causes of the stress that students, in particular ninth-grade students, experience?*

    Follow-up question:

    - *In addition to feelings of stress, what are the other primary challenges that ninth-grade students experience?*

7. *What is your understanding of the support and resources available to students experiencing stress and other challenges?*

    Follow-up questions:

    - *To your knowledge, how frequently do students use these resources?*
    - *Are these resources useful?*

8. *We understand that there is not a formal policy regarding making referrals, but is there an informal policy on who should recommend that a student consider seeking out help? For example, should the student's adviser make that recommendation? How does this process work in practice?*

    Follow-up question:

    - *Is there a time in which you recommended these resources to a student? If so, what happened?* (Again, students should not be mentioned by name.)

9. *Are there ways that the support and resources could be improved? If so, how?*

10. *Is there anything else you think we should know about this issue that we have not asked?*

Wrap-up

Thank you so much for your time. Please do not hesitate to reach out to us at any point if you have any questions or want to share additional information.

Notes

RESOURCE G:
Potential Aspects to Consider During School-Based Observations

Description of event: For example, you might be observing a second-grade classroom during a math lesson or the school yard during morning admission.

Number of individuals: Include the number of students, teachers, and others (specify) in the setting.

Relevant contextual factors: Consider things like school events, time of day, and the participants.

Important actions: For example, what are the students and teachers doing? What opportunities are available for students or teachers to engage in content?

Policies: What, if any, school policies are in effect?

Key stakeholders involved: Stakeholders can include students, parents, guardians, teachers, and community members.

Relationships between stakeholders: For example, how are parents interacting with teachers? How are students interacting with each other?

Leadership: Who is leading the event? Is leadership shared in any way?

Roles and responsibilities: For example, what are the students' responsibilities? The parents'? The teachers'?

Decision-making: Who is making decisions, and how?

Methods of communication: How do individuals or groups communicate with each other? How do they show their level of respect?

Physical space: What stands out about the physical space or location?

Trust: Is there evidence that stakeholders trust each other? That there is a lack of trust? Document this evidence.

Values: What values are evident? For example, how are individuals' actions representing their values?

School procedural elements: For example, how do students make the transition between classes?

Cultural considerations: Is there evidence of a school culture and subcultures? What are some examples of this culture and subcultures?

Shared understanding: Do you notice shared understanding about various issues, such as the ways to act in certain spaces versus others?

RESOURCE H:
Template for Open-Ended Fieldnotes Instrument

Teacher	
Observer	
Date and time	
Content area	
Lesson focus	
Grade	
Number of students	
Classroom arrangement (e.g., rows, tables, groupings)	
What I see and hear (Describe what you see and hear.)	
My interpretations (Try to separate judgments, opinions, and the like, from more descriptive observations. For example, the statement that students "look bored" is a judgment and would go in this column.)	

RESOURCE I:
Example of a Student Focus Group Instrument

Date	
Time	
Focus group facilitator	
Notetaker	
Participant names	
Location (E.g., classroom, district office, on phone)	
Have signed parental consent form	☐ Yes
Reviewed and signed assent form	☐ Yes
Consent to be audio-recorded	☐ Yes ☐ No
Opening script (This need not be read verbatim, a script is helpful to guide how you will begin the focus group.)	*Hello. For those of you who don't know me, my name is [name]. I am a [your position].* *The goal of this focus group is to understand what you're learning about in your reading and English classes and what you think about what you're learning. We have a few guiding questions, but the goal is for all of you to have a conversation with each other.* *There are a few norms we'd like to establish before we begin. First and most important, we need to be respectful of each other and to acknowledge that it's OK to disagree. We also need to have time to hear from everyone.* *Your parent or guardian has already signed a consent form online and given their consent that you can participate and that this focus group can be audio-recorded.* *You also signed an assent form. Participation is completely voluntary, and you do not have to answer any question, and you may stop participating at any time. Identifying information will not be shared, and we'll keep your information confidential.* *Finally, we ask that you keep what is shared in this focus group confidential.* *Do you have any questions for me before we begin?* *Okay. We have about ___ minutes for the focus group, and I'm now going to, with your permission, turn on the recorder.*

Questions

I'd like for everyone to take a few minutes to write down a couple of thoughts about our first question. The question is, What are you learning or have you learned in English class? This way, you can refer back to your thoughts as we begin our discussion.

1. *How would you describe what you are learning or have learned in English class?*
2. *Do you believe that what you are learning in English class is reflected on the [specific name] test you take? Explain how it is reflected or how it is not reflected on the test.*
3. *What is your favorite moment during an English class you have had at [school name]? Explain what makes this a favorite moment.*
4. *What is your least favorite part of English classes—either past or present? Explain why this is your least favorite part.*
5. *As eighth graders, you will be starting high school next year. Do you believe you are prepared for high school English classes? Explain why or why not.*
6. *What else should we know about your experiences or concerns in English class at [school name]?*

Wrap-up

Thank you so much for your time. Please do not hesitate to reach out to us at any point if you have any questions or want to share additional information.

Notes

RESOURCE J:
Example of a Survey Sent to Teachers

The goal of this brief survey is to help us better understand the way that our school approaches literacy instruction, both formally in reading and English classes and informally in all classes. This survey should take about fifteen minutes to complete. Your responses will be kept confidential. Please email Charles if you have any questions or concerns about the survey. Thank you for your time!

Literacy Instruction

(These questions will provide a sense of how you teach literacy.)

1. Is reading or English the primary subject you teach? *(Circle one)*

    Yes *(Go to question 2)*   No *(Go to question 3)*

2. If you answered yes, what is the primary goal you want your students to achieve in your classes? Please include an example of what this goal looks like on a daily basis in your classes.

3. If you answered no, how do you incorporate literacy (reading and writing) instruction in your subject areas? Please include an example of what this looks like in your classes on a daily basis.

Background Information

The responses to the survey will be anonymous. However, to get a better sense of your answer, we would like some background information to help us contextualize your responses.

4. What grade group represents your teaching? *(Circle one)*

    K–2   3–5   6–8   Specials teacher

5. What subject(s) do you teach? *(Check all that apply)*

    ☐ Art   ☐ English   ☐ Foreign language   ☐ Math   ☐ Music
    ☐ Speech and debate   ☐ Social studies   ☐ Reading   ☐ Science

6. How long have you been teaching? *(Circle one)*

    0–5 years   6–10 years   11–15 years   16–20 years   20+ years

Final Thoughts

7. Is there anything else we should know about your teaching practice related to teaching reading and writing?

RESOURCE K:
Sample Data Collection Plan and Timeline

TASK	PERSON(S) RESPONSIBLE	DATE
Quick research training on interviews	One or two team members with research experience	January 17–30, 2019
Develop interview instrument	James, Rupi, and Patricia	February 2
Develop focus group instrument	Maria and Karim	February 2
Group exercise: rehearse instruments	All	February–March
Refine interview instrument	James, Rupi, and Patricia (after two or three interviews have been conducted)	February 15
Refine focus group instrument	Maria and Karim (after two or three focus groups have been conducted)	February 15
Compose formative analysis memo (see chapter 6)	All team members	March 1
Transcribe (or fill in notes) for interviews	Person who conducted each interview Possibly ofice staff	After each interview (All interviews completed by March 20)
Transcribe (or fill in notes) for focus groups	Person who conducted each focus group Possibly ofice staff	After each focus group (All focus groups completed by March 20)
Create data summary forms for interviews & focus groups (see chapter 6)	Person who conducted each interview	After each interview/focus group (All forms should be completed by March 25)
Team discussion of interview & focus group findings	Rupi and Karim lead meeting	March 30

RESOURCE L:
Template for Aligning Methods to Research Questions

RESEARCH QUESTION	PARTICIPANTS	DATA COLLECTION METHOD	RATIONALE
Write one research question per row. Remember that you can revise your research questions.	What people or sources (e.g., students, parents, teachers, admins) will you collect data from for this research question?	How will you collect data for this research question (e.g., interviews, focus groups, observational fieldnotes, surveys)?	Why do you think these participants and methods will answer this question the best?

RESOURCE M:

Software Programs and Other Resources for Recording and Organizing Data

Transcription Services
There are many transcription services (e.g., Rev.com). They typically charge by the minute of audio to transcribe a file. Even when you use a transcription service, accuracy is not guaranteed. We recommend comparing the transcript with the audio file to check for accuracy. These services tend to be very fast. Rev.com, for example, sends the transcribed file back to you within twenty-four hours.

Other Devices and Software
With the proliferation of new software and apps, you can purchase a device or an app that will simultaneously record and transcribe. We have not personally used these tools, but many of our graduate students have done so. They report that these new tools are approximately 60 percent accurate.

Data Analysis Programs
There are many computer-assisted qualitative data analysis programs, for example, the internet-based Dedoose and the downloadable program Atlas.ti. These programs *do not analyze data.* They are primarily used to organize data, and they can facilitate coding processes, which are one part of a larger analytic process. Depending on the amount of data your team collects, using one of these programs (especially Dedoose, since it is web- rather than portal-based and allows for multiple users to be signed into the same project at once) might be something for your team to consider.

RESOURCE N:
Examples of Data Summary Forms

Personal Interview

Source of data	*Interview with Mr. Smith (pseudonym), fourth-grade teacher*
Data collected, reviewed by	*Sarah and James*
Date, time, and location of data collection or review	*May 3, 2019, 3:45–4:15 p.m., Mr. Smith's classroom*
Name of associated data file	*Smith_interview_20180503*
Date summary form completed	*May 4, 2019*
Person completing form	*Sarah*
Summary of data	*Mr. Smith expresses frustrations with teaching fourth grade because the students take multiple standardized state tests, including science, writing, reading, and math, in this grade. He notes that literacy skills are embedded in all these subjects and would like more support for teaching and engaging students in more critical thinking rather than feeling so much pressure to teach to the state tests.*
Lingering questions	*Is this a common concern among all teachers, fourth-grade teachers, or other new teachers like Mr. Smith?*
People to follow up with	*Mrs. Johnson, the fourth-grade lead teacher*
Potential themes, codes	*Critical thinking, teaching to the test, supporting teachers, teacher constraint*
Other notes, ideas	*Connection between the plateauing of scores and a frustration of teachers?*

Review of Existing Document

Source of data	*2018 Student Code of Conduct*
Data collected, reviewed by	*Micah, Selma, Marquis*
Date, time, and location of data collection or review	*April 15, 2019, conference room, 4:00 p.m.*
Name of associated data file	*student code of conduct_2018*
Date summary form completed	*April 17, 2019*
Person completing form	*Marquis*
Summary of data	*The current Student Code of Conduct emphasizes what students may not do (e.g., arrive late to class or vandalize school property). The document also outlines the consequences of not meeting these rules and expectations (e.g., parent-teacher conferences, in-school suspensions).*
Lingering questions	*Why don't we include information about who created this Code of Conduct? It feels like student voice is lacking. Why is this?*
People to follow up with	*Mr. Washington, the informal disciplinarian*
Potential themes, codes	*Student behavioral expectations, school consequences*
Other notes, ideas	*The Code of Conduct reads like a list of don'ts. We wonder how students and families learn about resources and supports that are available to them. In addition, we are wondering how more student voice could be incorporated into the Code of Conduct.*

RESOURCE O:
Example of a Code List and Definitions

Research question: How are professional development decisions made in the Arland School District?

CODE	DEFINITION
Needs	A decision or program addresses the needs of a group of constituents
Deficit orientation	Individuals are viewed in stereotypical or other negative ways
Finances	Referring to discussion of the district's or school's budget
Communication	Ways that district policies and programs are communicated internally and externally; ways that officials communicate with each other
Student expectations	The expectations regarding students; including expectations set by principals, teachers, and the students themselves
Rationale	The stated or implied rationales for professional development decisions
Student-centered	Discussion of decision-making revolves around a student-centered philosophy
Involvement of school personnel	The extent to which school personnel (principals, teachers, specialists) are involved in professional development decisions
Collaborative	Involving multiple groups of stakeholders in decision-making
Authoritative	Decisions are made by one or two individuals at the district office

RESOURCE P:
Example of a Data Analysis Plan

TASK	PERSON(S) RESPONSIBLE	DATE
Transcribe (or fill in notes) for interviews	Person(s) who conducted each interview	After each interview (all interviews completed by March 20, 2019)
Transcribe (or fill in notes) for focus groups	Person(s) who conducted each focus group	After each focus group (all focus groups completed by March 20)
Create data summary forms for interviews and focus groups	Person(s) who conducted each interview	After each interview, focus group (all forms completed by March 25)
Compose formative analysis memo	All team members	March 30
Team discussion of interview and focus group findings and formative analysis memos	Rupi and Karim lead meeting	March 30
Quick research training data analysis	One or two team members with research experience lead meeting	April 5
Develop codes and code definitions from formative analysis memos, data summary forms, existing literature, and team meetings; divide data among groups for reading and coding data	All team members, in groups during team meeting	April 12
Read and code data	All team members	April 20
Organize coded data, and determine new groups for reading and discussing the coded data	Team meeting on April 21, and then all team members in groups	April 21
Read coded data and refine or create new codes and themes (in preparation for the summative analysis memo)	All team members	April 30
Compose summative data analysis memo after reading and discussing the coded data and reviewing data summary forms and formative analysis memos	All team members (either individually or as a small group)	April 30
Discuss summative analysis memos in team meeting, and think about potential findings across all the data	All team members, one or two team members lead meeting	May 1
Finalize thematic analytical findings	All team members, one or two team members lead meeting	May 7

GLOSSARY

anonymity: the assurance that the identities of the research participants will remain completely unspecified in the final outputs of research. Anonymity means that no one can identify any individuals who participated in a study (e.g., 52 percent of the teacher participants rated their professional development as "highly useful"). In most applied research, anonymity is rare because of the small sample size and because qualitative data are not typically aggregated. We suggest instead that you ensure confidentiality rather than anonymity with your participants.

applied research team: a focused group of educational stakeholders who collaborate on ongoing research with the goal of improving some aspects of education at a local level. The type of research that these teams conduct has direct applications to a particular setting, such as a school, a district, or another educational organization. These teams meet regularly and are involved in ongoing learning processes, with the goal of applying their research findings to their local circumstances.

capacity building: broadly, the development of professional abilities and skills. In an organizational sense, capacity building refers to different ways to foster the development and enhancement of skills, knowledge, motivation, and positive learning experiences, with special consideration given to the resources that organizations and individuals need to be effective. Capacity building should proceed from a resource orientation that looks at the knowledge and skills that people already have rather than one that focuses on deficits, or what people lack.

coding: a systematic data analysis process where researchers assign labels or codes to portions of data to support a broader process of data analysis. Codes create focal areas of the data for continued reading and analysis and thereby reduce the data set to the portions of data that relate to the guiding research questions. Codes can consist of words or short phrases that describe the data or can represent an analytical concept.

community of practice: a self-identified and voluntarily formed group that brings colleagues (and possibly other stakeholders) together to work collectively toward a set of shared interests and goals. The communities of practice that we propose operate along the lines of an organization in which everyone is involved in continuous learning, and leadership is shared among multiple stakeholders.

confidentiality: in qualitative research, the researcher's promise to respect and attend to the value of preserving each participant's privacy; revolves around decisions about how and what participant data will be disseminated. In their data collection and reports, researchers will often change the participants' names and other identifying information to protect people's privacy.

data analysis: a series of processes in which researchers interpret and make sense of the data collected to respond to their research questions. Primary analysis activities in applied research include multiple readings of data, coding or labeling the data, analyzing codes, and developing themes and findings. We recommend that analysis be done through the convening of multiple processes of dialogic engagement.

data summary form: a template that research team members develop early on in the data collection process to represent data as they are collected. The form is completed after each data collection moment as a way to document ongoing data analysis. Each research team member writes a brief summary of what was learned during data collection and notes any other important information or questions that arose. These forms are then labeled and stored along with other data sources so that they can be shared with research team members.

deductive analytical approach: an approach that involves analyzing data according to an existing framework by applying preexisting concepts or theories to data. The primary goal of deductive analysis is to see if, and then how, these concepts or theories are present in the data you collected.

dialogic engagement: a term we coined for a process in which researchers intentionally engage with other people throughout a research project to benefit from dialogue and collaboration on research questions, design, data collection, and analysis. This collaboration helps teams both to include multiple perspectives and to challenge the perspectives of those on the team. Considering a range of perspectives and experiences different from your own is an important part of selecting collaborators.

emergent design: the changeable structure of a research scheme because of the fluid nature of research processes, which can evolve in response to the realities of any situation. The research needs to be responsive to the real-life learning that the team acquires throughout its research. The term *emergent* is also used in qualitative data analysis to signal when concepts emerge inductively, that is, come directly from the data rather than from a deductive approach.

empirical: based on qualitative, quantitative, or mixed-methods research. The scholarly literature often distinguishes between empirical (or research-based) studies and philosophical or conceptual studies, in which new ideas are put forth but are not necessarily centered on research-based data.

formative data analysis: analysis that happens while data are still being collected; similar to formative assessment. Using formative analysis, research team members can revise their instruments and share with other members what they are learning so far. The enhanced knowledge may lead to the pursuit of additional perspectives or data.

inductive analytical approach: a method that involves discovering patterns, themes, and concepts in data. With this approach, learning emerges directly from your engagement with the data rather than from assigning preexisting theories or concepts to the data as done in deductive coding. The primary goal of inductive analysis is to learn directly from the data.

informed consent and assent: verbal or written agreement to participate in a study. Potential participants must be informed about all aspects of a study before they agree to participate. Being informed means being made aware of any risks, how much time is involved, how their information will be used, and how (and if) their privacy will be protected. Consent can only be given by adults eighteen years or older. Because anyone under the age of eighteen cannot legally consent to participate in a study, parental consent must be obtained. However, researchers need to obtain *informed assent* from children as a means of respecting their personhood even if they cannot legally consent. To obtain assent, the researchers would explain to minors (in an age-appropriate way) what the study entails, what they will be asked to do, and that there are no penalties for refusing to participate or answer a question. Thus, informed assent is a way of getting their consent even if they cannot legally give it; that is why it is referent to as *assent*.

inquiry stance: a reflective learning position for oneself, in one's professional practice, and in the setting that shape that practice; a way of approaching work by continuously reflecting on and being curious about one's practice. To develop an inquiry stance on your practice, you must build a solid knowledge of the practice. Developing an inquiry stance can be thought of as a habit of mind, the habit being situating yourself as a curious learner and placing process and relationships (rather than being right or knowing everything) at the center; it also means valuing deep lifelong learning and seeing that learning comes from a range of sources.

mixed methods research: the strategic combination of qualitative and quantitative research through collecting, analyzing, and integrating quantitative and qualitative data in a single study. For example, researchers might use quantitative data to measure student academic results and apply qualitative data to interview teachers and students about these results.

problem of practice: a site-specific (e.g., specific to a classroom, a school, a district, or another setting) issue or problem that a team can work to better understand and then develop local, data-based solutions. For example, a teacher coach might examine how she can help first-year teachers incorporate formative assessments in their practice. This problem of practice stems from the teacher coach's local practice of working with first-year teachers.

photovoice: a qualitative data collection method borrowed from participatory research approaches; documents people's experiences and situations from many vantage points. The goal of this flexible process is to enable people to shed light on their lived realities and the situations that highlight the research themes. In photovoice, individuals take pictures to document topics and experiences through images. Photovoice is combined with narratives, wherein people tell their own stories of the pictures and explain what the images represent and why they chose them. In this way, the shared new perspectives raise awareness of hidden or overlooked issues or other aspects of the institution, community, and so on.

qualitative research: a method of observation and interviewing to gather nonnumerical data; refers to the meanings and other descriptions of things and not to their counts or measures. Broadly, qualitative research seeks to explore the lived experiences of individuals and groups as people conceptualize and describe them. Its primary values include a focus on context, interpretation, and representation. Qualitative research is also a subjective, or nonneutral, process: the researchers influence and are influenced by the research. Qualitative research approaches are employed across many academic disciplines, focusing particularly on the human elements of the social and natural sciences.

quantitative research: broadly, research designs in which variables are used to measure relationships. Quantitative methods emphasize objective measurements and the statistical, mathematical, or numerical analysis of data collected through surveys, polls, priority rankings, or manipulating preexisting statistical data with computational techniques.

reflexivity: a central concept in qualitative research; broadly conceived as systematic, ongoing yet focused reflection about how one's biases, identities, relationships to the setting and participants, and personal experiences influence aspects of the research. Reflexivity is a way of actively monitoring, often through the use of memos, how you are affecting the research you conduct.

research instrument: in qualitative research, a tool that researchers use to collect data related to the research questions and topic. For example, a researcher creates an *interview instrument* that lists a series of questions to be asked of a participant during an interview. Other examples of research instruments are an observational guide, a focus group instrument, and a list of survey questions.

research participants: the individuals who will be interviewed, surveyed, observed, or otherwise related to the data collected in a qualitative research study. Other terms that are used include *informants subjects*, but we prefer the use of the term *participants* as it acknowledges how all the individuals construct knowledge and meaning together.

researcher memos: tools used in qualitative research to document research processes and findings. In qualitative studies, researchers often compose memos about multiple topics, including research design, data collection, and data analysis. Research memos can be especially useful in group research, as they can be shared between team members. You can also write these memos to help yourself make meaning of your findings.

sampling: where the data will come from; usually includes decisions about who will participate in a study. These decisions can also be related to settings, events, or groups that will be included in the study. Qualitative researchers generally describe sampling decisions as *site and participant selection*, which includes where the study will take place and who will be involved.

validity: in qualitative and applied research, the assurance that the findings are faithful to the participants' experiences. You can enhance the validity of your applied research study in many ways. For example, you can conduct participant validation, incorporate multiple perspectives and data sources, engage in reflexivity, and use dialogic engagement.

NOTES

INTRODUCTION

1. Gary L. Anderson, "Reflecting on Research for Doctoral Students in Education," *Educational Researcher* 31, no. 7 (2002): 22–25; Sharon M. Ravitch and Susan L. Lytle, "Becoming Practitioner-Scholars: The Role of Practice-Based Inquiry Dissertations in the Development of Educational Leaders," in *Contemporary Approaches to Dissertation Development and Research Methods*, ed. Valerie Storey and Kristine Hesbol (Hershey, PA: IGI Global, 2016), 140–161.

CHAPTER 1

1. James H. Lytle, *Working for Kids: Educational Leadership as Inquiry and Invention* (Lanham, MD: Rowman and Littlefield, 2010).
2. Marilyn Cochran-Smith and Susan L. Lytle, *Inquiry as Stance: Practitioner Research for the Next Generation* (New York: Teachers College Press, 2009).
3. Joan Lave and Etienne Wenger, *Situated Learning: Legitimate Peripheral Participation* (Cambridge: Cambridge University Press).
4. Carol S. Dweck, *Mindset: The New Psychology of Success* (New York: Random House, 2006).
5. Susan Black, "Finding Time to Lead," *American School Board Journal* 187, no. 1 (2000): 46–48; Warren G. Bennis, *Why Leaders Can't Lead: The Unconscious Conspiracy Continues* (San Francisco: Jossey-Bass, 1989); Amy C. Edmondson, "The Competitive Imperative of Learning," *Harvard Business Review*, July–August 2008, 60–67.
6. Peter Senge, "The Leader's New Work: Building Learning Organizations," *Sloan Management Review* 32, no. 1 (1990): 7–23.
7. See, for example, Sharon M. Ravitch and Nicole Mittenfelner Carl, *Qualitative Research: Bridging the Conceptual, Theoretical, and Methodological* (Thousand Oaks, CA: Sage, 2016); Barry C. Jentz and Jerome T. Murphy, "Embracing Confusion: What Leaders Do When They Don't Know What to Do," *Phi Delta Kappan* 86, no. 5 (2005): 358–66; James H. Lytle, *Working for Kids: Educational Leadership as Inquiry and Invention* (Lanham, MD: Rowman and Littlefield, 2010); Noel M. Tichy and Nancy Cardwell, *The Cycle of Leadership: How Great Leaders Teach Their Companies to Win* (New York: Harper Business, 2002); Senge, "The Leader's New Work."
8. Marilyn Cochran-Smith and Susan L. Lytle, *Inquiry as Stance: Practitioner Research for the Next Generation* (New York: Teachers College Press, 2009).

9. Roland S. Barth, *Improving Schools from Within: Teachers, Parents, and Principals Can Make the Difference* (San Francisco: Jossey-Bass, 1990).
10. Cynthia E. Coburn and Erica O. Turner, "The Practice of Data Use: An Introduction," *American Journal of Education* 118, no. 2 (2011): 99–111.
11. Stephen J. Ball, "The Teacher's Soul and the Terrors of Performativity," *Journal of Education Policy* 18, no. 2 (2003): 215–28; Jal Mehta, "How Paradigms Create Politics: The Transformation of American Educational Policy, 1980–2001," *American Educational Research Journal* 50, no. 2 (2013): 285–324.
12. See, for example, Barth, *Improving Schools from Within*, 9; Senge, "The Leader's New Work."
13. Cochran-Smith and Lytle, *Inquiry as Stance*; Jean Lave and Etienne Wenger, *Situated Learning: Legitimate Peripheral Participation* (Cambridge, UK: Cambridge University Press, 1991).
14. Gordon A. Donaldson Jr., "What Do Teachers Bring to Leadership?" *Educational Leadership* 65, no. 1 (2007): 26–29.
15. Sally Jacoby and Patrick Gonzales, "The Constitution of Expert-Novice in Scientific Discourse," *Issues in Applied Linguistics* 2, no. 2 (1991); Michael van Manen, *Researching Lived Experience* (New York: State University of New York Press, 1990); Lee S. Shulman, *The Wisdom of Practice: Essays on Teaching, Learning, and Learning to Teach* (San Francisco: Jossey-Bass, 2004).
16. Richard Elmore, "Agency, Reciprocity and Accountability in Democratic Education," in *The Institutions of American Democracy: The Public Schools*, ed. Susan Fuhrman and Marvin Lazerson (Oxford: Oxford University Press, 2005), 277–301.
17. See, for example, Ball, "The Teacher's Soul"; Gary Anderson and Michael I. Cohen, "Redesigning the Identities of Teachers and Leaders: A Framework for Studying New Professionalism and Educator Resistance," *Education Policy Analysis Archives* 23, no. 85 (2015): 1–23.
18. Anderson and Cohen, "Redesigning the Identities."
19. Anderson and Cohen, "Redesigning the Identities."
20. See, for example, Mark A. Bautista et al., "Participatory Action Research and City Youth: Methodological Insights from the Council of Youth Research," *Teachers College Record* 115, no. 10 (2013): 1–23.
21. Kimberlé W. Crenshaw, "Mapping the Margins: Intersectionality, Identity Politics, and Violence Against Women of Color." *Stanford Law Review* 43, no. 6 (1991): 1241–99.
22. Barth, *Improving Schools from Within*.
23. Richard R. Valencia, *Dismantling Contemporary Deficit Thinking: Educational Thought and Practice* (New York: Routledge, 2010).

CHAPTER 2

1. Frederick Erickson, "Culture in Society and in Educational Practices," in *Multicultural Education: Issues and Perspectives*, ed. J. A. Banks and C. A. M. Banks (Hoboken, NJ: Jossey-Bass, 2004), 31–60.
2. Erickson, "Culture in Society"; Sonia Nieto, *Affirming Diversity: The Sociopolitical Context of Multicultural Education* (New York: Longman Press, 2004).
3. Edward H. Schein, *Organizational Culture and Leadership*, 5th ed. (San Francisco: Jossey-Bass, 2016).

4. James H. Lytle, *Working for Kids: Educational Leadership as Inquiry and Invention* (Lanham, MD: Rowman and Littlefield, 2010).
5. Lytle, *Working for Kids*.
6. Michael J. Nakkula and Sharon M. Ravitch, eds., *Matters of Interpretation: Reciprocal Transformation in Therapeutic and Developmental Relationships with Youth* (San Francisco: Jossey-Bass, 1998).
7. See, for example, Dan C. Lortie, *Schoolteacher: A Sociological Study* (Chicago: University of Chicago Press, 1975).
8. Gareth Morgan, *Images of Organization* (Thousand Oaks, CA: Sage, 2006).
9. Howard C. Stevenson, *Promoting Racial Literacy in Schools: Differences That Make a Difference* (New York: Teachers College Press, 2014).
10. Derald Wing Sue, *Microaggressions and Marginality: Manifestation, Dynamics, and Impact* (Hoboken, NJ: John Wiley and Sons, 2010).
11. Stevenson, *Promoting Racial Literacy in Schools*.
12. Stevenson, *Promoting Racial Literacy in Schools*.
13. Stevenson, *Promoting Racial Literacy in Schools*.
14. Stevenson, *Promoting Racial Literacy in Schools*.
15. Kimberlé W. Crenshaw, *On Intersectionality: Essential Writings* (New York: New Press, 2019).
16. See, for example, Marc A. Brackett, Susan E. Rivers, and Peter Salovey, "Emotional Intelligence: Implications for Personal, Social, Academic, and Workplace Success," *Social and Personality Psychology Compass* 5, no. 1 (2011): 88–103.

CHAPTER 3

1. See, for example, Joseph A. Maxwell, *Qualitative Research Design: An Interactive Approach*, 3rd ed. (Thousand Oaks, CA: Sage, 2013); Sharon M. Ravitch and Nicole Mittenfelner Carl, *Qualitative Research: Bridging the Conceptual, Theoretical, and Methodological* (Thousand Oaks, CA: Sage, 2016).
2. Maxwell, *Qualitative Research Design*.
3. Ravitch and Carl, *Qualitative Research*; Maxwell, *Qualitative Research Design*.
4. Maxwell, *Qualitative Research Design*.
5. Colin Robson, *Real World Research*, 3rd ed. (Oxford: Blackwell, 2011); Edgar H. Schein, *Organizational Culture and Leadership*, 3rd ed. (San Francisco: Jossey-Bass, 2004).
6. Kimberlé W. Crenshaw, "Mapping the Margins: Intersectionality, Identity Politics, and Violence Against Women of Color," *Stanford Law Review* 43, no. 6 (1991): 1241–99.
7. Crenshaw, "Mapping the Margins."
8. Nicole Mittenfelner Carl and Sharon M. Ravitch, "Member Check," in *The SAGE Encyclopedia of Educational Research, Measurement, and Evaluation*, ed. Bruce B. Frey (Thousand Oaks, CA: Sage, 2018), 1,050; Ravitch and Carl, *Qualitative Research*.
9. Ravitch and Carl, *Qualitative Research*.
10. Nicole Mittenfelner Carl and Peter Kuriloff, *Factors that Mediate YPAR Effectiveness*, midyear evaluation report, Center for the Study of Boys' and Girls' Lives, University of Pennsylvania (2017); Peter Kuriloff and Nicole Mittenfelner Carl, *Assessing the Necessary Conditions for*

Effective YPAR, midyear evaluation report, Center for the Study of Boys' and Girls' Lives, University of Pennsylvania (2016).
11. See, for example, Nancy Fichtman Dana, *Leading with Passion and Knowledge: The Principal as Action Researcher* (Thousand Oaks, CA: Corwin, 2009).
12. Dana, *Leading with Passion and* Knowledge.
13. Ravitch and Carl, *Qualitative Research*.
14. Rick Mintrop, *Design-Based School Improvement: A Practical Guide for Education Leaders* (Cambridge, MA: Harvard Education Press, 2016).
15. See, for example, Sara Efrat Efron and Ruth Ravid, *Action Research in Education: A Practical Guide* (New York: Guilford Press, 2013).

CHAPTER 4

1. Sally Jacoby and Patrick Gonzales, "The Constitution of Expert-Novice in Scientific Discourse," *Issues in Applied Linguistics* 2, no. 2 (1991); Max van Manen, *Researching Lived Experiences* (Albany: State University of New York Press, 1990).
2. Richard DuFour et al., *Learning by Doing: A Handbook for Professional Learning Communities at Work*, 3rd ed. (Bloomington, IN: Solution Tree Press, 2016); John Dewey, *Democracy and Education* (New York: Simon & Brown, 1916); David A. Kolb, *Experiential Learning: Experience as the Source of Learning and Development*, 2nd ed. (London: Pearson Education, 2015).
3. Richard Elmore, "Agency, Reciprocity and Accountability in Democratic Education," in *The Institutions of American Democracy: The Public Schools*, ed. Susan Fuhrman and Marvin Lazerson (Oxford: Oxford University Press, 2005), 277–301.
4. Jon R. Katzenbach and Douglas K. Smith, *The Wisdom of Teams: Creating the High-Performance Organization* (Boston: Harvard Business Review Press, 1993).
5. Richard R. Valencia, *Dismantling Contemporary Deficit Thinking: Educational Thought and Practice* (New York: Routledge, 2010).
6. Lee S. Shulman, *The Wisdom of Practice: Essays on Teaching, Learning, and Learning to Teach* (San Francisco: Jossey-Bass, 2004).
7. Henry A. Giroux, *Teachers as Intellectuals: Toward a Critical Pedagogy of Learning* (New York: Bergin and Garvey, 1988).
8. The discussion of brave spaces was inspired by Brian Arao and Kristi Clemens, "From Safe Spaces to Brave Spaces: A New Way to Frame Dialogue Around Diversity and Social Justice," in *The Art of Effective Facilitation: Reflections from Social Justice Educators*, ed. Lisa M. Landreman (Sterling, VA: Stylus Publishing, 2013), 135–50.
9. Arao and Clemens, "From Safe Spaces to Brave Spaces."
10. Arao and Clemens, "From Safe Spaces to Brave Spaces."
11. See Howard C. Stevenson, *Promoting Racial Literacy in Schools: Differences That Make a Difference* (New York: Teachers College Press, 2014).
12. Katzenbach and Smith, *The Wisdom of Teams*.
13. Katzenbach and Smith, *The Wisdom of Teams*.
14. Mario Moussa, Madeline Boyer, and Derek Newberry, *Committed Teams: Three Steps to Inspiring Passion and Performance* (Hoboken, NJ: John Wiley and Sons, 2016).

15. Moussa, Boyer, and Newberry, *Committed Teams*.
16. Moussa, Boyer, and Newberry, *Committed Teams*.
17. Mark Hannum, "The Toxic Effects of Communication Triangulation," *Leadership Insights* (blog), *Leverage*, August 15, 2015, http://blog.linkageinc.com/blog/systems-thinking-5-the-toxic-effects-of-communication-triangulation.
18. Arao and Clemens, "From Safe Spaces to Brave Spaces."

CHAPTER 5

1. Robert. S. Weiss, *Learning from Strangers* (New York: Free Press, 1994).
2. Michael Q. Patton, *Qualitative Research and Evaluation Methods*, 4th ed. (Thousand Oaks, CA: Sage, 2015), 444–45.
3. Colin Robson, *Real World Research*, 3rd ed. (Oxford: Blackwell, 2011); Edgar H. Schein, *Organizational Culture and Leadership*, 3rd ed. (San Francisco: Jossey-Bass, 2004).
4. Harry F. Wolcott, *Transforming Qualitative Data: Description, Analysis, and Interpretation* (Thousand Oaks, CA: Sage, 1994).

CHAPTER 6

1. Sharon M. Ravitch and Nicole Mittenfelner Carl, *Qualitative Research: Bridging the Conceptual, Theoretical, and Methodological* (Thousand Oaks, CA: Sage, 2016).
2. William J. Gibson and Andrew Brown, *Working with Qualitative Data* (Thousand Oaks, CA: Sage, 2009).
3. Urie Bronfenbrenner, *The Ecology of Human Development: Experiments by Nature and Design* (Cambridge, MA: Harvard University Press, 2009).
4. Matthew B. Miles, A. Michael Huberman, and Johnny Saldaña, *Qualitative Data Analysis: A Methods Sourcebook* (Thousand Oaks, CA: Sage, 2014).
5. Virginia Braun and Victoria Clarke, "Using Thematic Analysis in Psychology," *Qualitative Research in Psychology* 3, no. 2 (2006): 77–101.
6. See Ravitch and Carl, *Qualitative Research*, for more detail about developing findings.

CHAPTER 7

1. Derald Wing Sue, *Microaggressions and Marginality: Manifestation, Dynamics, and Impact* (Hoboken, NJ: John Wiley and Sons, 2010).

RESOURCES

1. Thank you to Taylor Hausburg for reviewing and synthesizing this material.

ACKNOWLEDGMENTS

Books are the result of many minds and much collaboration. In this spirit, we deeply appreciate the following people for their direct hand in helping us with this book and for their support throughout (and beyond) the book-writing process.

Thanks to our editor, Caroline Chauncey, for your vision, constructive feedback, and steadfast support throughout the book development and writing. And for so respectfully pushing us to make the book stronger at every step of the way. Thank you to Christopher Leonesio for supervising the copyediting, design, and composition of our book. Thanks to Patricia Boyd for excellently copyediting the manuscript. You helped us communicate our ideas more effectively and succinctly. We also thank all the individuals at Harvard Education Press who supported the production and marketing of our book, including Laura Cutone Godwin, Christina DeYoung, and Rose Ann Miller.

Susan and Torch Lytle, thank you for your ongoing grounding and inspiration about inquiry in practice, assets-based school improvement, and the generation of local data to drive sustainable educational change. Thanks to Peter Kuriloff, our longtime colleague and friend with whom we have had many important discussions about applied research. Katie Pak, thanks for your generative insights throughout this project and your detailed feedback on many chapters. Taylor Hausburg, we are grateful for your continued support on multiple aspects of the book's development. Sherry Coleman and Ari Burstein supported us in the development of examples and visuals.

Sharon's Thanks

Thank you, Nicole, for being my thought partner in our work, in this book, and in life! You are brilliant, and your way of thinking and doing both inspires and grounds me. You're a truly incredible woman, friend, colleague, comrade, and writing partner. I adore, value, and respect you beyond words. You are a marvel!

To the hardworking doctoral students in three programs—Mid-Career Doctorate in Educational Leadership, Chief Learning Officer, and Executive Doctorate in Higher Education Management—at the University of Pennsylvania Graduate School of Education, thank you for teaching me how qualitative research can be used to change the world. And for your questions and applications of ideas in practice!

My wonderful colleagues at Penn with whom I teach and collaborate: Michael Nakkula, Howard Stevenson, Annie McKee, Matt Hartley, Susan Yoon, Dana Kaminstein, Mike Johanek, Kathy Rho, Peter Eckel, Elliot Weinbaum, Stephanie Levin, Matt Riggan, Leslie Nabors-Oleh, Laura Perna, Marsha Richardson, Charlotte Jacobs, Jere Behrman, Kandi Wiens, Devesh Kapur and Penn's Center for the Advanced study of India (CASI), Peter Kuriloff, Kate Windsor, and Chris Soto—thank you for teaching, supporting, and inspiring me. And big appreciation goes to Pam Grossman, dean of the Graduate School of Education, for your ongoing support.

My colleagues around the world, who teach me things beyond what I could articulate: Dr. Venkatesh Kumar, at the Tata Institute of Social Sciences in Mumbai, thank you for your thought and action partnership, your openness to co-learning, and your friendship. Thank you to Shambhavi Singh and rohan sarma for your incredible generosity of intellect and spirit. Deep appreciation to Ishita Roy of India's Ministry of Human Resource Development. Gowri Ishwaran, educator par excellence in Delhi, thank you for your energy and our ongoing partnership. Duilio Baltodano, of the Seeds for Progress Foundation in Managua, Nicaragua, you have been a comrade in our work and a dear friend for almost a decade. Creutzer Mathurin and Sergot Jacob in Port-au-Prince, Haiti, thank you for continuing to walk our complicated and vital path together, *Avè w map mache*. Melissa DePino, I am grateful for your friendship and everyday thought partnership, especially on our morning walks—you always #ShowUp (@privtoprog)!

I thank my early and ongoing mentors, who walk and have walked with me throughout my career: Carol Gilligan, Fred Erickson, Sara Lawrence-Lightfoot, Joe Maxwell, and Meg Turner. Each of you taught me to view the world in ways that elevate me, my work, and, I hope, the people around me. Ruthy Kaiser, thank you for helping me reframe and understand myself and the world. I am grateful for my good fortune to personally engage with Paulo Freire and Audre Lorde; those conversations keep me working toward a humanizing approach to research.

My sons, Ari and Lev, and my ex-husband and best friend, Andy, thank you for your love, your care, and your support of my career and engaging with my ideas and work. My parents, Arline and Carl Ravitch, you are a pillar of strength for me, and your steadfast support is my wind. My siblings, Frank Ravitch and Elizabeth Ravitch, and my Uncle Gary, who embodies the kindness of my grandparents, Edith and Albert Karp (z"l), thank you for keeping me rooted and always encouraging me. Laura Ellen Hoffman, Deborah Melincoff and Hooman Yaghoobzadeh, Melissa DePino, Amy Leventhal and Marc Diamond, Susan and Torch Lytle, Perri Shaw Borish, as well as Anne, Sydney, and Gabe Rogers—you sustain me!

My students, you teach and nourish me every day. Some garden I teach! Thank you for your questions, humor, engagement, resonance, strong questioning spirits, and energy! Several students have had and continue to have a significant impact on my thinking and research: Matthew Tarditi, Laura Colket, Katie Pak, Iván Rosales Montes, Sherry Coleman, Arjun Shankar, Dave Almeda, Viju Menon, Kelsey Jones, Adrianne Flack, Reima Shakeir, Serrano LeGrand, Rich Liuzzi, Taylor Hausburg, Amber Daniel, Jerry Maraia, Jasmine Blanks, Janay and James Garrett, A. J. Schiera, Chris Steel, Melinda Bihn, Christiana Kallon-Kelly, Christa Bialka, Oreoluwa Badaki, David DeFilippo, Susan Feibelman, Leland McGee, James Arrington, Vikas Joshi, Tina Arrington, Wagner Marseille, Robert McGarry, and Anuba Tyagi.

Nicole's Thanks

Sharon, you provided steadfast thought partnership, inspiration, friendship, and comedic relief throughout the writing of this book as well as across all our work together. Thank you for your continued support and mentorship in everything I do. I look forward to a lifetime of collaboration with you.

My students at University of Pennsylvania Graduate School of Education challenge me, ask so many thoughtful questions, and push my learning in new directions. I am especially thankful to my students who are also educators. I hope you know how much I value all the hard work you do every day to make our world a better place.

I thank my colleagues at Penn GSE and other places, in particular Peter Kuriloff, Stephen Sacchetti, Venkatesh Kumar, Philippe Bourgois, Rand Quinn, Jessica Watkin, A. J. Schiera, Justice Walker, Charlotte Jacobs, Christopher Dean, Howard Stevenson, Kelsey Jones, Taylor Hausburg, Shambhavi Singh, Dana Kaminstein, Joseph Nelson, and Katie Pak.

To my husband, Jason, and to my mother, Iva Linda, thank you for continued support throughout my life and in particular for helping me make time for the writing of this book. And to my children, Evey and Max, thanks for the way you look at, question, and have faith in the world.

ABOUT THE AUTHORS

SHARON M. RAVITCH is a professor of practice at the University of Pennsylvania's Graduate School of Education. Ravitch engages in numerous applied research projects in India, serving as a visiting scholar at the Tata Institute of Social Sciences (TISS) in Mumbai and working as a co-researcher and key resource expert in policy advocacy, professional development, and community-based participatory research related to corporate social responsibility through TISS's Corporate Social Responsibility Hub. She is involved in the design and implementation of assessment and evaluation of statewide performance through mixed methods research in the Ministry of Human Resource Development's major policy initiative, Rashtriya Uchchatar Shiksha Abhiyan (RUSA), a countrywide reform initiative aimed to resurrect India's state public university system. Ravitch is also an expert adviser at the Center for Academic Leadership and Education Management at TISS. The center provides professional development and policy advocacy support to school education leaders across India. Ravitch works in the center's capacity-building program to collaboratively develop case studies and technology-innovation frameworks for the higher education and K–12 sectors using a participatory approach. She received the prestigious GIAN Scholar Award from the government of India for 2016–2017 and the RUSA Scholar Award for 2017–2018. Ravitch also received a Fulbright Fellowship to engage in research and applied development work in India from 2017 to 2019.

Ravitch is also principal investigator of Semillas Digitales, a multiyear applied development research initiative in rural Nicaragua that is a partnership with the Seeds for Progress Foundation. Ravitch's research integrates across the fields of qualitative research, education, applied development, cultural anthropology, and human development and has four main strands: (1) practitioner research for sustainable, stakeholder-driven professional and institutional development and innovation; (2) international applied development research that works from participatory and action research approaches (projects currently in India and Nicaragua); (3) ethnographic and participatory evaluation research; and (4) leader inquiry, education, and professional development.

Ravitch has published four books: *Qualitative Research: Bridging the Conceptual, Theoretical, and Methodological* (with Nicole Carl, 2016). *Reason and Rigor: How Conceptual Frameworks Guide Research* (with Matthew Riggan, 2016); *School Counseling Principles: Diversity and Multiculturalism* (2006); and *Matters of Interpretation: Reciprocal Transformation in Therapeutic and Developmental Relationships with Youth* (with Michael Nakkula, 1998).

Ravitch earned two master's degrees from Harvard University, one in risk and prevention and another in human development and psychology, and a doctorate from the University of Pennsylvania in an interdisciplinary program that combined education, anthropology, and sociology.

NICOLE MITTENFELNER CARL is a postdoctoral fellow in the Teaching, Learning, and Leadership division at the University of Pennsylvania Graduate School of Education. She received her doctorate in educational leadership from the University of Pennsylvania in 2017. Carl teaches courses related to qualitative research methods, practitioner research for educational leaders, and mentoring strategies for veteran teachers coaching first-year teachers.

Carl's research has three primary foci: (1) professional development and coaching for teachers and leaders, (2) how practitioners and students can conduct research to improve their schools, and (3) the social and cultural contexts of schooling and its implications on students, teachers, parents, and school leaders.

Carl has been conducting qualitative research for more than a decade, beginning in 2005, when she was awarded a Mellon Fellowship. Since then, she has led and participated in numerous qualitative and mixed-methods research projects and written a seminal text with Sharon Ravitch about qualitative research methods: *Qualitative Research: Bridging the Conceptual, Theoretical, and Methodological* (2016). She has also published several articles on students' experiences with schooling, the impacts of educational policies on teachers and leaders, and applied research in peer-reviewed journals.

Carl has worked with school leaders, teachers, and students in various settings (public and independent) to consider ways to use research to drive school improvement. She has also led a multiyear, multisite evaluation of the impact of these projects on the schools and the individuals involved. She continues to research ways that practitioners can conduct and use research in their schools, and she supports schools in the implementation of these projects.

Drawn from her experiences as a teacher, a teacher leader, and a teacher coach, Carl's current research, a multiyear ethnographic study of a K–8 school in a low-income neighborhood in a large urban city, describes the ways that hidden agendas of social class immobility and inequity shape schooling experiences. The research examines socialization structures in schools, the role of cultural and social capital, the importance of qualitative research, ways to incorporate student voice, and how policy is experienced by students and teachers.

INDEX

accountability
   government policies for, 19
   shared, of research team, 21, 69, 71, 87, 88, 97, 127
action plan
   barriers to, 172
   components of, 171–172
   including stakeholders in, 172–174
   reflection and follow-up of, 174–175
administrators. *see* educational leaders
analysis of data. *see* data analysis
analytical approaches
   deductive, 145–146, 210
   inductive, 145–146, 211
analytic findings. *see* research findings
analytic memos. *see also* memos
   formative analysis memos, 128, 140–141
   summative analysis memos, 149–150
analytic themes. *see* themes
anonymity
   defined, 209
   of participants, 63, 65, 116–117, 170
   of team members' comments, 97
applied research
   benefits and goals of, 2–4, 162–163, 179–182. *see also* action plan; professional development
   defined, 1–3, 11–14
   designing. *see* research design
   examples of. *see* examples
   findings from. *see* research findings
   instruments for. *see* research instruments
   methods for. *see* research methods
   participants for. *see* research participants
   questions for. *see* research questions
   resistance to, overcoming, 39–45
   topic for. *see* research topic
applied research team
   capacity building for, 87–88
   collaboration of. *see* collaboration
   defined, 91, 209
   dialogic engagement of, 67, 68–69, 128, 210
   dynamics in, 88–89, 95–97
   goals of, 93
   mindsets beneficial to, 81–86
   norms in, 94–95
   roles in, 93–94
   safe and brave spaces for, 38, 89–91, 99–100
   shared accountability of, 21, 69, 71, 87, 88, 97, 127
   size of, 91–92
   who should be included in, 39, 92
archival data. *see* preexisting data
assumptions about research topic, 130
audio recordings
   capturing in notes or transcripts, 64, 111–112, 138

audio recordings, *continued*
   of focus groups, 111–112
   of interviews, 107–108
   participant permission for, 107, 111
   resources for, 138

biases and blind spots, 98–99, 126–127. *see also* reflexivity
brave spaces, 38, 89–91, 99–100

capacity building, 87–88, 209. *see also* professional development
change. *see* organizational change
coded data
   analyzing, 146–149
   compared to findings, 153
   compared to themes, 149
coding
   assigning codes, 142–146
   based on terms in literature, 143, 145, 156
   changing codes, 148
   defined, 209
   resources for, 143
collaboration
   data analysis using, 159–160
   fostering, 20–21, 24–25
   mindsets beneficial to, 81–86
   as professional development, 180
   on research topic and goals, 50–52
   on thematic findings, 151–153
collection of data. *see* data collection
communication
   observing, 32
   safe and brave spaces for, 38, 89–91, 99–100
community members. *see* applied research team; educational stakeholders
community of practice
   as applied research team, 11, 20–21, 85
   defined, 11, 209–210
   inquiry stance for, 10–11
   learner stance for, 17
conceptual teaching practices, 154–158, 171
confidentiality, 65, 110, 210
culture, organizational. *see* organizational culture

data, existing. *see* preexisting data
data analysis
   coding, 142–146, 148, 209
   collaborative workshops for, 159–160
   data summary form for, 141–142, 210
   deductive, 145–146, 210
   defined, 136, 210
   formative, 128, 139–141, 211
   inductive, 145–146, 211
   plan for, 158–159
   processes in, 136–137
   recording data, 137–138
   resources for, 158
   summative, 141–150
   systematic, 75, 136
   thematic findings from, 141, 150–154
data collection
   formative analysis during. *see* formative data analysis
   instruments for. *see* research instruments
   methods for. *see* research methods
   multiple forms of, using, 120–123
   plan for, 129
   research questions determining, 104–105, 129
   resources for, 129
   sampling for, 64–67, 76, 104–105, 213
   storing and organizing data, 64, 138–139
   systematic, 75
   timeline for, 129
   validity of data, ensuring, 68, 123–128
data summary form, 141–142, 210

Index   231

deductive analytical approach, 145–146, 210
deductive codes, 143
design, research. *see* research design
dialogic engagement, 67, 68–69, 128, 210
discussion questions
   about norms, 34–35
   about organizational culture, 32–33
district data, preexisting, 58

educational leaders
   applied research benefitting, 2–3
   capacity building, developing in others, 87–88
   collaboration, fostering, 20–21, 24–25
   defined, 4
   learner stance, developing, 17–18, 23–24
   practices for. *see* practices
   qualitative research, consideration of, 18–20, 24
   status quo, challenging, 21–23, 25–26
educational stakeholders
   in communities of practice, 10–11, 20–21
   dissemination of findings to, 163–165
   including in action plan, 172–174
   involving in research, 39–40, 44, 45–46, 71, 83–84, 91
   perspectives on organizational culture, 31–32, 38, 42
emergent design, 74–75, 210
empirical research, 55, 60, 77, 210
employee data, preexisting, 58
equity and identity
   assessing, 32, 36–38
   safe and brave spaces for discussing, 89–91, 99–100
ethical considerations
   anonymity, 63, 116–117, 170
   confidentiality, 110, 210
   informed consent or assent, 63, 107, 211
   list of, 65–66
   privacy, 63, 110, 170

examples
   conceptual teaching practices, 154–158, 171
   data analysis, 154–158
   data collection, multiple forms of, 120–123
   developing findings, 151–153
   disseminating research findings, 163–168
   interview instrument, developing, 109
   literacy instruction, 59–62, 113, 120–123, 144, 147–148, 151–153
   mapping, 118–120
   organizational change, overcoming resistance to, 40–45
   participant validation, 123–127
   preexisting data, research design using, 59–62
   research team dynamics, 95–97
   school accreditation and applied research, 72–73
   student behavior, 85–86
   student discipline policy, 14–16, 163–168
   students consistently late to school, 12
   student suspensions, 54, 56–57, 64, 74
existing knowledge. *see also* preexisting data
   defined, 76
   memos for, 77–78
   review of, 55–58, 78, 120–121
   sources of, 54–55
   using in research design, 59–62
existing-knowledge memos, 77–78
external policies, 19, 35–36

fieldnotes
   context information in, 114
   defined, 62, 64
   jottings as first step of, 112, 113
   neutrality in, 113–114
   sharing with team members, 123
   systematic process for, 112

findings. *see* research findings
fishbowl exercises, 131–132
flash focus groups, 46
focus groups
    audio recordings of, 111–112
    defined, 110
    flash focus groups, 46
    informing participants prior to, 110
    notes from, 46, 111–112
    questions for, 110–111
    rehearsing, 111
    resources for, 122
    semistructured, 110
focus walks, 45–46
formative analysis memos, 128, 140–141
formative data analysis
    data summary forms for, 141–142
    defined, 128, 139, 211
    documenting, 128, 140–141

goals, research. *see* research goals
government policies, 19, 35
growth mindset, 16, 18, 23. *see also* learner stance; organizational change

identity. *see* equity and identity
individualism, 33
inductive analytical approach, 145–146, 211
inductive codes, 143
informed action, 73–74, 77. *see also* organizational change
informed consent or assent, 63, 65, 107, 211
inquiry stance, 10–11, 211
institutional change. *see* organizational change
institutional culture. *see* organizational culture
instruments, research. *see* research instruments

intersectionality, 37–38
interviews
    audio recordings of, 107–108
    defined, 105–106
    informing participants prior to, 107
    notes from, 64, 108, 111–112
    questions for, 54, 106–107, 108–109
    rehearsing, 108
    resources for, 109
    semistructured, 106

jottings, 112, 114

leaders, educational. *see* educational leaders
learner stance, 10–11, 17–18, 23–24, 180, 181
literacy
    instruction, research example, 59–62, 113, 120–123, 144, 147–148, 151–153
    racial and identity-based, 37–38
literature review, 55–56, 78, 120–121

mapping, 118–120
memos. *see also* notes
    existing-knowledge memos, 77–78
    formative analysis memos, 128, 140–141
    mini memos, in formative analysis, 140
    mini memos, in reflexivity, 126–127, 130
    of others' fieldnotes, 123
    researcher memos, 212
    summative analysis memos, 149–150
    topic-exploration memos, 75–77
methods, research. *see* research methods
microaggressions, 36
mindsets
    capacity building, 87–88
    collaboration, fostering, 20–21, 24–25
    growth mindset, 16, 18, 23

learner stance, developing, 17–18, 23–24, 84–86
multiple perspectives, valuing, 82–84
openness to change, 18, 41–43, 73–74, 86
qualitative research, consideration of, 18–20, 24
status quo, challenging, 21–23, 25–26
mini memos
  in formative data analysis, 140
  in reflexivity, 126–127, 130
mission statement, 38–39
mixed-methods research, 3, 211

neutrality
  in fieldnotes, 113–114
  in research questions, 53
norms, 33–35, 94–95. *see also* roles
notes. *see also* memos
  of audio recordings, 64, 111–112, 138
  of dialogic engagement, 128
  of focus groups, 46, 111–112
  of interviews, 64, 108, 111–112
  of observations (fieldnotes), 62, 64, 112–114, 123, 132
  of participant validation, 125
  of photovoice debriefings, 117–118
  of preexisting data reviews, 61
  of town hall meetings, 96

observations
  of classroom, overcoming resistance to, 33–34
  of communication, 32
  of emotions and attitudes, 32
  fieldnotes from, 62, 64, 112–114, 123, 132
  participant observation, 112
  resources for, 113
openness
  to change, 18, 41–43, 73–74, 86

  to other perspectives, 10, 17, 20–21, 25, 34–35, 82–84, 93, 99, 100
organizational change
  as goal of applied research, 162
  openness to, 18, 41–43, 73–74, 86
  planning for, 73–74
  resistance to, overcoming, 39–45
  sustaining, 162, 174–175, 176–177, 179–182
organizational culture
  action plans for, 171–175
  assessing, 31–36
  defined, 31
  discussion questions regarding, 32–33
  dynamic nature of, 31, 39
  equity and identity, 32, 36–38
  importance to applied research, 30–31
  of individualism, 33
  mission and vision statements, 38–39
  multiple perspectives of, 34–35
  norms, 33–35
  policies, 33–34, 35, 38–39
  roles, 35–36
  values, 31, 38–39
organizational data, preexisting, 58
organizing data, 64, 138–139

parents. *see* educational stakeholders; research participants
participants. *see* research participants
perspectives, multiple
  for data sources, 57, 68, 125–126
  openness to, 10, 17, 20–21, 25, 34–35, 82–84, 93, 99, 100
  for organizational culture, 34–35
  for participants, 23, 53, 67–68, 82–84, 110, 117, 121–123, 125–126
  for team members, 25, 39, 81, 83–84, 92, 93, 96, 125–126
photovoice, 117–118, 212
policies
  external, 19, 35–36

policies, *continued*
   government, 19
   organizational, 33–34, 35, 38–39
   school discipline, 14–16, 163–168
power dynamics, 88–89
practice, community of. *see* community of practice
practice, problem of. *see* problem of practice
practices
   biases and blind spots, assessing, 98–99
   brave spaces, creating, 99–100
   collaboration, fostering, 20–21, 24–25
   collaborative data analysis workshop, 159–160
   data analysis plan, 158–159
   data collection aligned to research questions, 129
   data collection plan and timeline, 129
   existing-knowledge memo, 77–78
   fishbowl exercises, 131–132
   flash focus groups, 46
   focus walks, 45–46
   learner stance, developing, 17–18, 23–24
   list of, 183
   ongoing systematic reflection, 176–177
   qualitative research, consideration of, 18–20, 24
   reflexivity through mini memos, 130
   research design template, 76–77, 78
   research instruments, refining, 130–132
   status quo, challenging, 21–23, 25–26
   topical professional development, 175–176
   topic-exploration memo, 75–77
praxis, 176–177
preexisting data. *see also* existing knowledge
   applied research building on, 57–62, 76
   data summary forms for, 141–142
   reading and coding, 142, 146
   relevance of, 115, 122

reviewing, 61, 115, 120–121
   types of, 55, 57–58
principals. *see* educational leaders
privacy, 63, 65, 110, 170
problem of practice, 15, 52, 211
professional development, 3, 71, 171–172, 175–176, 179–182. *see also* capacity building

qualitative research
   consideration of, 18–20, 24
   defined, 3, 212
   narrowed focus and context for, 53–54
   quantitative data used with, 3
   reflexivity with. *see* reflexivity
quantitative research
   data from, using with qualitative approaches, 3
   defined, 212
   limitations of, 19
questions
   about norms, 34–35
   about organizational culture, 32–33
   for interviews, 54, 106–107, 108–109
   research questions. *see* research questions

race
   equity and identity, 32, 36–38
   racial literacy, 37
   racial microaggressions, 36
   racial stress, 36–37, 174
recording data, 137–138
reflexivity
   defined, 68, 81–82, 124, 212
   practices for, 98–100, 130
   as validity process, 126–128
research, types of. *see* applied research; mixed-methods research; qualitative research; quantitative research

research design
  defined, 50–51
  emergent, 74–75, 210
  existing knowledge, examining, 54–62, 76, 77–78
  informed action, planning for, 73–74, 77
  methods, determining, 62–64, 76
  participants, selecting, 64–67, 76
  questions for, determining. *see* research questions
  resources for, 78
  systematic processes in, 75
  template for, 76–77, 78
  time and resources, allocating, 69–73, 77
  topic and goals, determining, 50–52, 75–77
  validity, ensuring, 67–69, 76
researcher memos. *see also* memos
  defined, 140, 212
  formative analysis memos, 128, 140–141
  summative analysis memos, 149–150
research findings
  action plans resulting from, 171–175
  audiences of, planning for, 74, 168–169
  compared to codes and themes, 153
  in data summary forms, 141
  defined, 150
  developing collaboratively, 151–153
  disseminating, 163–170
  dissemination plan for, 163–165
  maintaining openness to, 73–74
  number of, 150–151
  ongoing systematic reflection on, 176–177
  professional development from, 175–176
  quotes supporting, 153
  relationship to research questions, 154
  relevant literature supporting, 168, 170
  structure and format for, 168–170
  validity of, 213
research goals, 50–52, 54, 75–77
research instruments
  defined, 104, 212
  fieldnotes, 62, 64, 112–114, 123, 132
  focus group questions, 110–111
  interview questions, 106–107, 108–109
  modeling, 131–132
  observational guide, 113
  piloting, 131
  rehearsing, 131
  research questions determining, 104–105
  survey questions, 115–117
  vetting, 130–131
research methods
  focus groups, 46, 110–112
  interviews. *see* interviews
  list of, 105–106
  mapping, 118–120
  observations. *see* observations
  permissions required for, 63
  photovoice, 117–118
  preexisting data, reviewing, 61, 115, 120–121
  research questions determining, 104–105, 129
  selecting, 62–64, 76
  sequencing of, 63
  surveys, 115–117
research participants
  anonymity of, 63, 65, 116–117, 170, 209
  confidentiality of, 65, 110, 210
  defined, 14, 212–213
  diversity of, 67
  indicating in organized data, 148
  informed consent or assent of, 63, 65, 107, 211
  informing of focus group process, 110
  informing of interview process, 107
  participant observation, 112
  permission for audio recordings, 107, 111
  privacy of, 63, 65, 110, 170
  sampling (selecting), 64–67, 76, 104–105, 213
  validation of, 67–68, 123–127

research questions
    changes to, during a study, 52, 104
    data collection aligned to, 104–105, 129
research questions, *continued*
    developing, 52–54, 76
    findings related to, 150, 154
research team. *see* applied research team
research topic, 50–52, 75–77, 130
resource and time allocation, 69–73, 77
resources in this book
    audio recordings, 138, 203
    biases and blind spots, 99, 193
    coding, 143, 206
    data analysis, 158, 207
    data collection, 129, 201, 202
    data summary form, 141, 204
    flash focus groups, 46, 188
    focus groups, 122, 198
    focus walks, 46, 187
    interviews, 109, 194
    observations, 113, 196, 197
    research design, 78, 191
    safe and brave spaces, 38, 185
    surveys, 122, 200
    transcripts, 138, 203
roles. *see also* norms
    assessing, 35–36
    defined, 35
    selecting participants based on, 66–67

safe spaces, 89–90. *see also* brave spaces
sampling, 64–67, 76, 104–105, 213
school data, preexisting, 58
semistructured focus groups, 110
semistructured interviews, 106
small-group discussions. *see* flash focus groups
stakeholders. *see* educational stakeholders
stances. *see* mindsets
status quo, challenging, 21–23, 25–26

stories from the field. *see* examples
storing data, 64, 138–139
stress
    racial and identity-based, 36–37, 174
    researching, example of, 109
students. *see also* educational stakeholders; research participants
    focus groups of, 121–122
    preexisting data regarding, 58
    student discipline policy, example researching, 14–16, 163–168
    students late, example researching, 12
    student suspensions, example researching, 54, 56–57, 64, 74
summary form. *see* data summary form
summative analysis memos, 149–150
summative data analysis
    analyzing coded data, 146–149
    defined, 141–142
    documenting, 149–150
    reading and coding data, 142–146
    thematic approach for, 141
superintendents. *see* educational leaders
surveys
    anonymity in, 116
    data analysis of, 116
    defined, 115–116
    demographics in, 116–117
    questions for, 115–117
    resources for, 122
systematic processes, 75, 112, 136, 176

tags. *see* coding
teachers. *see* applied research team; educational leaders; educational stakeholders; research participants
team. *see* applied research team; community of practice
template for research design, 76–77, 78
thematic analysis, 141

thematic findings. *see* research findings
themes
   compared to codes, 149, 153
   documenting, 149–150
   finding in data, 140–141, 142, 145
theoretical research, 1, 55, 60, 77
time and resource allocation, 69–73, 77
timeline for research, 70
topic, research. *see* research topic
topic-exploration memos, 75–77
town hall meetings, 96, 173
transcripts
   of focus groups, 111–112
   of interviews, 64
   resources for, 138

tyranny of numbers, 3. *see also* government policies; quantitative research

validity
   defined, 67, 213
   dialogic engagement for, 68–69, 128
   multiple data sources and perspectives, 68, 125–126
   participant validation, 68, 123–125
   processes ensuring, list of, 67, 76
   reflexivity for, 68, 126–128
values, 31, 38–39
vision statement, 38–39